Philosophy and Artificial Intelligence

Todd C. Moody

St. Joseph's University

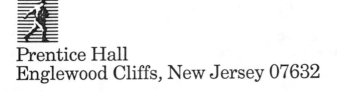

Prentice Hall
Englewood Cliffs, New Jersey 07632

Library of Congress Cataloging-in-Publication Data

Moody, Todd C.
    Philosophy and artificial intelligence / Todd C. Moody.
        p.   cm.
    Includes index.
    ISBN 0-13-663816-3
    1. Philosophy of mind—Data processing. 2. Philosophy—Data
processing. 3. Artificial intelligence.   I. Title.
BD418.3.M66   1993
128'.2—dc20   92-6206
                                                            CIP

Acquisitions editor: **Ted Bolen**
Editorial/production supervision and interior design: **Jordan Ochs**
Editorial Assistant: **Diane Schaible**
Copyeditor: **Mark Stevens**
Prepress buyer: **Herb Klein**
Manufacturing buyer: **Patrice Fraccio**
Cover design: **Rich Dombrowski**

 ©1993 by Prentice-Hall, Inc.
A Simon & Schuster Company
Englewood Cliffs, New Jersey 07632

Printed in the United States of America
10 9 8 7 6 5 4 3 2 1

ISBN   0-13-663816-3

Prentice-Hall International (UK) Limited, *London*
Prentice-Hall of Australia Pty. Limited, *Sydney*
Prentice-Hall Canada Inc., *Toronto*
Prentice-Hall Hispanoamericana, S.A., *Mexico*
Prentice-Hall of India Private Limited, *New Delhi*
Prentice-Hall of Japan, Inc., *Tokyo*
Simon & Schuster Asia Pte. Ltd., *Singapore*
Editora Prentice-Hall do Brasil, Ltda., *Rio de Janeiro*

Contents

3
Computing Machines   **47**

4
The Turing Test   **75**

5
The Nature of Intelligence   **101**

6
Connections   **129**

Preface

It is inevitable that students, instructors, and general readers interested in learning about the intersection of philosophy and artificial intelligence will approach the subject with different levels of background knowledge of either component. Some will be familiar with philosophy but will know little about computers, let alone artificial intelligence. For others the situation will be reversed. Since I intend this book to be an introduction to the subject, I have avoided presupposing that the reader has an extensive background in philosophy or artificial intelligence. Highest priority has been given to accessibility of the material.

At the same time, I wanted the volume to be compact, to enhance its usefulness. In an introductory philosophy course, the instructor might wish to spend some time examining the philosophical problems of artificial intelligence, in which case this book could be used as an adjunct to other course texts. In a course in the philosophy of mind, the instructor would wish to delve more deeply but might nevertheless find the book useful as a starting point. By the same token, instructors of courses in artificial intelligence might want their students to be acquainted with the philosophical aspects of their work.

It is worth emphasizing that this is a *philosophy* book. As such, it focuses on philosophical rather than technical issues. The technical issues and theories are an area of rapid development and change. New texts and new editions appear on the shelves each month. For reasons discussed in the Introduction, philosophical issues are a more slowly moving target. In the end, it is my hope that this book can give the reader an appreciation of the interdependence of the two domains and a desire to learn more.

I wish to thank St. Joseph's University for the Summer Research Grant that I received in 1989. This made it possible for me to think through some of the ideas for the book and to prepare a very rough draft.

Todd C. Moody

For Connie, Moira, and Dylan

What the hammer? What the chain?
In what furnace was thy brain?

—WILLIAM BLAKE
The Tyger

Chapter 1

Introduction

Philosophy "of" Anything

It is a matter of perennial dispute whether there is any real progress in philosophy. Skeptics, many of whom are or were students in philosophy classes, complain that the philosophers of the twentieth century are discussing essentially the same questions that their predecessors were discussing thousands of years ago. Some would go further and claim that they are also coming up with the same answers. Whitehead's famous remark that all of Western philosophy consists of "footnotes to Plato" was certainly not intended to disparage the discipline, but there are many—even within the community of academic philosophers—who see it as a condemnation.

Science, on the other hand, is generally regarded as the very emblem of progress. Certainly, there are disputes within and between the sciences, but there is something about those disputes that leads not just to a profusion of theories but to a *succession* of theories. There seem to be mechanisms or practices within the sciences for the replacement of a given theory by a better theory. We see the concrete traces of this succession in the expansion of technology.[1] It is not surprising that many would argue that science has superseded philosophy, which lingers on as

---

1. It is only fair to point out that everything that I have just said about science has been the subject of vociferous disagreement for decades. The disagreement, however, is not for the most part within the community of scientists; it is within the community of philosophers of science.

a quaint intellectual relic of a prescientific age. When a working scientist says of some problem or theory, "Let the philosophers worry about that," she suggests that the matter is not only beyond the resources of scientific methods, but also beyond the radius of what is worthy of serious attention. Let the philosophers worry about it, for all the difference it will make.

This attitude is based upon a caricature of what philosophy and science are all about. To an extent, that caricature is supported by the institutional fact that philosophy is an independent academic discipline, with its own university departments, courses, professional organizations, and journals. Despite this fact, I would like to sketch a different view of philosophy, a view that will help to put the subject matter of this book into perspective. It will also go some way toward answering questions that many people—including computer scientists—are inclined to ask: What business does a philosopher have writing a book about artificial intelligence? What could he possibly have to contribute?

According to my own view of things, philosophy is *not* a separate intellectual discipline, except in the most superficial institutional sense already noted. Instead, philosophy is the study of foundational issues and questions in whatever discourse (scientific, literary, religious, and so forth) they arise. The foundational issues are hard to define in a way that makes sense across all discourses. Still, if a given proposition is presupposed by all or most of the principal theories and methods of a discipline,[2] it is probably foundational. It would be fair to say that the foundations of a discipline are the concepts and principles most taken for granted in it. In mathematics, for example, a foundational proposition would be, "There are sets." The philosopher of mathematics might or might not want to deny this proposition, but would certainly want to ask in a rigorous way what it means.

Continuing with the mathematics example, most mathematicians are not interested in asking whether there are sets, or what it means

---

2.   Or discourse. A distinction could be made between discourses and disciplines, but it would not contribute much to the thread of this discussion.

to say that there are sets. They are interested in defining sets and using them to get on with specific research programs. There are nevertheless some mathematicians who are interested in just such foundational questions. In my view, these individuals are doing philosophy, whether they see themselves in this way or not. In fact, they are doing "philosophy of mathematics."[3] The fact of the matter is that many of the people who do philosophy of mathematics are in mathematics departments and many are in philosophy departments. To the people working in this area, it is less important what department you are in than whether you have something to say that is interesting. Similar points can be made about the philosophy of biology, religion, or literary criticism.

If we take seriously these comments about the nature of philosophy, as well as the earlier comments about the profusion of disagreements in philosophy, we are led to the conclusion that within a given discipline, such as mathematics, there is less agreement about the foundations than there is about other matters. I believe this to be true. If the sciences are indeed the paradigms of progress, they achieve this status by somehow bypassing the foundational questions or, as was said earlier, by taking certain foundations for granted. This works well until a foundational proposition is directly challenged in some nonfoundational research. Determinism—the doctrine that each event is completely determined by causes—was not seriously questioned in physics until the quantum theorists needed to come up with a theory of what appeared to be spontaneous radioactive decay. Then the philosophy of physics became a prominent area of interest for some of the world's leading physicists. The practical rule in the sciences seems to be: Avoid confronting foundational questions until the avoidance blocks further progress. It's an unstated rule, but it appears to work well.

So the point is that philosophy is part of every serious inquiry or discipline. It would take us too far from the subject matter of this book to give careful consideration to the question whether philosophy ought

---

3. In fact, this area of study is one that mathematicians call "foundations of mathematics."

to exist as an autonomous discipline. But I would point out that what might be called the "logic" of foundational questions is not always so different from one discipline to another, even if the particulars are very different. Philosophy has developed a detailed understanding of that logic and a highly tuned sensitivity to the traps that await the unwary. There is every reason to see value in the preservation and development of this understanding, in conjunction with the development of the "philosophy of" this or that discipline or discourse.

The philosophy of mind is one of the most fascinating of all domains of philosophical inquiry. It's fascinating because there is nothing that is at once so mysterious yet central to the human condition as the fact that we have minds. We are not simply objects in this universe; we are also *subjects*. We occupy or embody a point of view. The philosophy of mind begins with astonishment at this fact and proceeds to an inquiry into how it is possible. You now understand that it is nonsense to suppose that the inquiry somehow *belongs* to the discipline of philosophy and not to some other discipline. The "philosophy of mind" is what philosophers call their own interest in foundational questions about the mind, but they are not the only ones who are interested. Psychologists, biologists, theologians, mathematicians, and many others who probably do not consider themselves philosophers may nevertheless be vitally interested in precisely the same questions. What I am calling the "philosophy of artificial intelligence" lies at the intersection of philosophy, psychology, linguistics, computer science, neuroscience, and logic. The dynamics of this collaboration are not always completely friendly. Certain philosophical conclusions may be unwelcome or even unacceptable to the scientist, who may insist that she is the only one *qualified* to have an opinion. This is especially likely when philosophers pass harsh judgment upon some research program and its alleged findings. I think it is important to keep in mind at such junctures that the critical task of philosophy should be understood as troubleshooting, not troublemaking. But here, too, the line can be blurry.

The reason for these introductory comments is that I want it to be clear that this is not a book written by a philosopher strictly for the eyes of other philosophers or even strictly for philosophy students. While such works lie at the heart of every discipline, I believe that there is also a need for works that mark and even strengthen the connections between disciplines. In addition, I think it is important that at least some works should be accessible to a general readership without sacrificing careful reasoning.

Artificial Intelligence: The Nickel Tour

Although later chapters discuss a number of aspects of artificial intelligence in detail, it is worthwhile to set out an overview of the subject at the beginning, so that the reader will be able to identify the most prominent points of the terrain. In particular, many people are confused as to the relation between artificial intelligence and the rest of computer science; some even take them to be synonymous, which they are not.

Even to say what a computer is raises some surprisingly subtle questions, which I will postpone until a later chapter. For purposes of introduction, it is enough to point out that the first clear example of a computer was Charles Babbage's "Difference Engine," a machine for calculating logarithms. Later, there were adding machines.[4] The first adding machines, such as those in cash registers, were built on mechanical principles. That is, the discrete states of an adding machine are actually the particular states of various ratcheted wheels and levers. Such machines could do nothing *but* add, for the most part, although more sophisticated versions were eventually built.

It is worth noting that adding machines were not called "computers" even though the word "compute" had certainly been around for a long time. Furthermore, it was apparently not a matter of much philosophical interest whether adding machines "really" add, or only seem to. You could think of them as machines that add, or as machines that people use when they do addition; nothing much seemed to be at stake in the distinction.

The first machine identified as an electronic computer was "Colos-

---

4. Earlier, if you count the abacus as an adding machine. It is not, however, an *automated* adding machine.

sus," a British machine designed by the mathematician Alan Turing (of whom we shall have more to say later) and built in 1943. Colossus was used to decipher German codes during World War II. This machine is described as electronic because its discrete states were defined not in terms of the positions of wheels, but rather in terms of the states of circuits of vacuum tubes. A point should be made here about the deciphering of codes that Colossus is alleged to have done. It is tempting to imagine an encrypted message being typed into the machine, which would hum or blink for a few seconds and then print out a nicely decoded message in German or, better, English. This is not how it was. It would be more correct to say that Colossus was used to perform rapidly and accurately the long and numerous computations needed to determine the code that the Germans were using.

Next was ENIAC, built at the University of Pennsylvania in 1946. This was an acronym for "electronic numerical integrator and computer." Like Colossus, ENIAC was a physically imposing object. It had 18,000 vacuum tubes and weighed about fifty tons. At a press-conference demonstration, ENIAC multiplied a five-digit number by itself 5,000 times in under a second. It was "programmed" to do this stunt by being wired in a certain way; if a different sort of computation was needed, it had to be rewired by hand.

The tasks that Colossus and ENIAC were used to perform—addition and multiplication—were not in themselves difficult to conceptualize, although it was (and still is) daunting to imagine computations being done so rapidly and accurately. The jargon for this sort of application is "number crunching"—performing lengthy or numerous arithmetical operations in a very short period of time. Number crunching is not in itself artificial intelligence. This observation should be kept in mind, since one might be tempted to think, "I can't do arithmetic nearly as quickly or accurately as this machine, and arithmetic is one of the things that you need intelligence for, so this machine must be more intelligent than I am."

While it is true that arithmetic is the sort of thing that people have traditionally associated with intelligence, it is not the sort of thing that the artificial-intelligence community has claimed as an achievement because it is only the *quantity* of the computer's operations that is remarkable. In itself, adding a couple of numbers is not particularly subtle or interesting.[5] Still, it is worthwhile to point out, even at this early stage of our exploration, that we have here a small sign of divergence of the meaning of the word "intelligence," as it is used in artificial intelligence, from its ordinary use. In a later chapter, the subtleties of the concept of intelligence will be examined in much greater detail.

Also in 1946, an important paper by the mathematician John von Neumann appeared. In this paper, von Neumann showed that a computing machine could be made to perform different sequences of operations without being rewired by hand. Instead, it could accept and store instructions coded in some numerical form; the sequence of operations would depend upon the instructions encoded in this "program." By 1948 the first stored-program computer had been built, in Manchester, England. This was a watershed point in the history of computing, since it now became possible to dissociate to some extent the programming of the computer from the physical principles of its operation. This permitted an explosion in the possible ways that computers could be used.

It was also in 1948 that the first chess-playing computer was built, at MIT. If we are looking for a single accomplishment to mark the start of artificial intelligence, this is a plausible choice. Chess playing is a good candidate because it has long been regarded as the province of the intelligent. Moreover, chess playing was virtually chosen in advance as a criterion of artificial intelligence, by the poet and essayist Edgar Allan Poe. In 1836 Poe wrote an essay entitled "Maelzel's Chess-Player" in *The Southern Literary Messenger*. Although automated computers were unheard of at that time, J.N. Maelzel (also inventor of the musician's metronome) had exhibited a device that consisted of a cabinet within which, when its doors were opened, could be glimpsed some elaborate machinery: metal wheels, rods, levers, and the like densely packed into a small space. On the cabinet a chessboard could be set up, and next to it was an artificial human figure—dubbed "the Turk"—with a movable

---

5. Having said that, I should point out that the *way* in which a computer handles an operation apparently as uninteresting as addition can be subtle indeed.

left arm. At an exhibition, the arm would move the chess pieces and play a creditable game of chess.

In his essay, Poe argued that Maelzel's machine could not be what it was alleged to be. His arguments include numerous observed grounds for suspicion that a concealed human midget was making the moves. What is more interesting, however, is that he also argued that no purely mechanical apparatus could *in principle* play the game of chess. Comparing chess playing to the sort of logarithmic calculations performed by Babbage's "Difference Engine," Poe wrote,

> Arithmetical or algebraical calculations are, from their very nature, fixed and determinate. Certain *data* being given, certain results necessarily and inevitably follow. These results have dependence upon nothing, and are influenced by nothing but the *data* originally given. And the question to be solved proceeds, or should proceed, to its final determination, by a succession of unerring steps liable to no change, and subject to no modification. . . . But the case is widely different with the Chess-Player. With him there is no determinate progression. No one move in chess necessarily follows upon any one other. From no particular disposition of the men at one period of a game can we predicate their disposition at a different period.[6]

The argument is clear enough. Since at any point in the course of a chess game (more accurately, *almost* any point) more than one move is possible, there is no relation of necessity between one board position and the next. In the absence of such a relation, a *choice* must be made, and this takes the matter outside of the realm of the mechanical. This, at least, was Poe's view.

It should not be thought that Poe's argument would apply only to those systems that are mechanical in the sense of being nonelectronic (a distinction that Poe himself could have had no glimmer of), even though he assumed (in a different passage) that the Chess-Player was supposed

---

6. Edgar Allan Poe, "Maelzel's Chess-Playing Machine, *Southern Literary Messenger*, April, 1836; reprinted in *The Portable Poe*, ed., Philip Van Doren Stern (New York: Penguin Books, 1977), pp. 511-12.

to be a "pure machine." The following passage leaves little room for doubt:

> It is quite certain that the operations of the Automaton are regulated by *mind* and by nothing else. Indeed this matter is susceptible of a mathematical demonstration, *a priori*.[7]

Poe believed that it could be proved in the strictest mathematical sense of the term that it takes a *mind* to play chess, because a mind can make choices that are not necessitated by prior circumstances. Of course, today you can walk into a toy store and buy an electronic gadget that will play a decent game of chess. This makes possible three replies to Poe: Either he was just wrong and you don't need a mind to play chess or he was right and these machines therefore have minds of some sort. The third possible reply is that the machines don't *really* play chess but only *simulate* it. We shall look closely at all three replies in later chapters.

For the record, the term "artificial intelligence"[8] was coined by John McCarthy in 1956 at a conference at Dartmouth College that may be regarded as the formal starting point of the artificial-intelligence movement. The purpose of the conference was stated in the application for the Rockefeller Foundation grant that supported it:

> The study is to proceed on the basis of the conjecture that every aspect of learning or any other feature of intelligence can in principle be so precisely described that a machine can be made to simulate it.[9]

One of the central philosophical problems that follows closely upon the heels of this "conjecture" (this word seems disingenuously modest) is to understand the relation that exists between the exact *simulation* of a

---

7. Ibid., p. 513.
8. The abbreviation "AI" is widely used now, both in writing and speech. I shall use it, too, where compactness of expression seems especially desirable.
9. Pamela McCorduck, *Machines Who Think* (San Francisco: W. H. Freeman, 1979), p. 93.

process and its actual *implementation* or *instantiation*. A strong claim is that the relation is identity.

In addition to McCarthy, three other key participants at the Dartmouth conference were Marvin Minsky, Allen Newell, and Herbert Simon. All four were to become leading figures in the artificial-intelligence movement. Artificial intelligence was officially on the intellectual map. Within a year, the programming language LISP (from "LISt Processing") was created. Other so-called "high-level" programming languages, such as FORTRAN (from "FORmula TRANslator"), were already in existence. The purpose of these languages was to make it easier for humans to program computers. Before high-level languages, the program instructions had to be coded in "machine language," which is the actual set of binary codes used by the machine. To construct complex algorithms and represent them in machine language is a difficult and error-prone process. A high-level language allows the programmer to write instructions in a form that looks at least something like English. Those instructions are translated into machine language by an intermediate program called a *compiler* or an *interpreter*.[10] LISP was the first high-level language created specifically for research in artificial intelligence.

In 1965, Joseph Weizenbaum published an article entitled "ELIZA—A Computer Program for the Study of Natural Language Communication between Man and Machine,"[11] in which he described a program that, in the form of typed output, simulated the responses of a nondirective psychotherapist. This program, about which I shall have much more to say in later chapters, was a milestone in the history of artificial intelligence for several reasons. First, it was the first well-known example of modestly successful "communication" between humans and computers in a natural language such as English. Second, even though ELIZA's "success" in this regard was quite modest, the program was immediately taken seriously as a prototype for serious future automated psychotherapists. Third, seeing the enthusiastic reception that ELIZA received in

---

10.   These are not the same, but the difference does not concern us here.

11.   *Communications of the Association for Computing Machinery*, 9, no. 1 (January 1965), 36-45.

some quarters, Weizenbaum himself became a leading skeptic in the artificial-intelligence community. His skepticism was not aimed at questioning the possibility of achieving certain goals, such as automated psychotherapists and teachers, but at the *wisdom* of pursuing such goals in the first place. We shall consider his views in detail in the last chapter of this book.

Another interesting development at MIT was Terry Winograd's program SHRDLU, created in 1970. Winograd was a doctoral student, and SHRDLU was a program that manipulated blocks according to instructions given by the user of the program. Because of its manipulative and instruction-following abilities, SHRDLU was a forerunner of later inventions in the field of *robotics*. As significant as this may be, the really interesting thing about SHRDLU was not its ability to play with actual blocks but its ability to follow instructions. Indeed, some imple-mentations of SHRDLU did not actually use physical blocks and robot arms. In these versions, SHRDLU manipulated "virtual" blocks in a universe that existed only in the computer's memory. (Much more recently, one hears such a universe described as a "cyberspace.")

It may seem that the ability to follow instructions was no great breakthrough, given that high-level programming languages had already existed for some time. SHRDLU was different, however. It followed instructions given in English and could answer simple questions about the "block-world." Furthermore, it would interact with the user to disambiguate instructions when necessary. If you typed in "Pick up the red block," it might reply "Which red block?" If you typed in an instruction or question that was somehow inconsistent with the arrangement of objects in the block world, it would inform you of the fact. The success of SHRDLU and other programs like it stimulated debate on the question whether such programs could really be said to understand the instructions and questions presented to them.

It may be worth pausing here to give the reader some sense of the positions in such a debate. Winograd's program had to incorporate a number of fairly sophisticated features. It had to have an internal representation, or model, of the block-world. It also had to have a "parser" that could analyze the sentences given to it and correctly identify their structural parts. Finally, it had to be able to map the meanings of those sentences somehow onto the features of the block-world, change the block-world when appropriate, and compose its own reply sentences. Described abstractly in this way, it certainly sounds as though the system understands. At the same time, its "understanding" is severely limited to the block-world. Some have argued that no system that is so severely limited deserves to be called a system that understands. After all, the argument goes, you and I understand in part what it means to pick up a block partly by virtue of understanding what things are *not* blocks and what block manipulation has to do with anything else. In short, our understanding of blocks is always embedded in a *context*, and that is precisely what SHRDLU lacks any cognizance of. A parallel argument can be offered against the claim that computers "understand" the game of chess. Can you understand the game of chess without also understanding what is *not* the game of chess, or without understanding what a game is in general? These questions will be taken up in later chapters.

Roger Schank, then of Yale University, pursued a line of research that attempted to extend the success of Winograd's work. Recognizing that SHRDLU's "understanding" was limited to the conceptual domain of the block-world, Schank tried to formalize the notion of context into a construct that he called a *script*. A script comprises background knowledge and assumptions about a certain kind of situation. If you are told, for example, that a man in a restaurant sent his untouched food back to the kitchen and got up and left, you might readily respond "No" to the question "Did he pay for his meal?" Even though you were not told that he didn't pay, you understand that, in the context of restaurants, when somebody sends food back it means that they found the food unacceptable, and when that happens they typically don't pay. Schank would say that you activate a restaurant script, and your understanding of the question put to you is partially determined by the contents of that script. M. G. Dyer, an AI researcher who works with some of Schank's ideas, developed a program called BORIS, which the philosopher Margaret Boden describes as follows:

BORIS's knowledge-base concerns such matters as adultery and divorce, and the emotional and legal tangles they may involve. Given the sentence "Paul wanted the divorce, but he didn't want to see Mary walk off with everything he had," this enables it to interpret "walk off with" as meaning possession rather than perambulation, and to see Paul's distaste for this prospect as a natural reaction to his discovery of his wife's infidelity. Moreover, BORIS assumes that Paul's emotion will lead him to adopt certain strategies rather than others, in virtue of the program's stored representation of the origin and psychological functions of various affects.[12]

There are variations on the script approach; similar strategies that were independently developed were characterized as "frames" or "microworlds." On this view, the problem of understanding in general is the problem of having enough frames and the right links between them. Critics, such as Hubert Dreyfus, charge that there is no reason to suppose that this approach will ever get beyond the "toy domain" stage, owing to the complexity and interdependence of the conceptual maps involved in "real" understanding. After all, the script about restaurants has to have links to other scripts about eating, paying for things, tipping, and so on. Part of understanding is having these links in place.

From the earliest days of artificial intelligence, there was a deep difference of opinion about the viability of two fundamentally different approaches. Although terminology varies, I describe these as the *symbolic processing* and *connectionist* approaches, in a chapter devoted to just this issue. In the symbolic-processing approach, the programmer creates an explicit representation of the "task-world," whatever it might be, in the computer's memory, in the form of some sort of a *data structure*. She then constructs an algorithm for manipulating the objects in that representation in ways that are supposed to be just like the ways objects interact in the real world domain of which the data structure is a representation. Connectionism, on the other hand, opts for a more implicit way of representing the task-world. Instead of modeling the world in a data structure, the programmer allows variable strengths of

---

12. Margaret Boden, *Computer Models of the Mind* (Cambridge: Cambridge University Press, 1988), p. 126.

interaction between submodules to represent the task-world and the system's interactions with it. The representation is implicit rather than explicit, although the notion of an "implicit representation" is itself controversial. The chapter on connectionism takes a closer look at these issues.

I have no illusion that these few sentences about symbolic-processing and connectionism make matters clear. These are perhaps the most difficult ideas in this book. I think they will be clearer when considered in context and spelled out more carefully. For now, it is sufficient to point out that until recently the symbolic-processing approach has dominated the field. All of the "milestone" projects mentioned so far have used this approach.

Another aspect of intelligence that has challenged AI researchers is learning. There is one sort of learning at which computers have excelled from the very beginning: the simple acquisition of information. This most trivial form of learning is usually described as *input*. One might even question my inclusion of simple input as a kind of learning, however rudimentary. The reason for doing so is that it satisfies at least one basic criterion of learning: the modification of a system's internal state to represent information external to it. On this understanding, human perception itself is a form of learning. More challenging, from the standpoint of artificial intelligence, is the acquisition and improvement of a skill.

Consider the chess-playing machines. They play a good game, but do they get better the more they play? Do they learn from their mistakes? Most of the commercially available ones do not. Interestingly, one of the earliest artificial-intelligence projects did have this capability. It was a checkers-playing program, created by Arthur Samuel of IBM (later of Stanford University) in 1947, when electronic computers were first being built. His program adjusted the weights of "values" it assigned to certain moves, depending upon whether or not they were successful. As it played more games, its own game became stronger.

A much-discussed recent example of machine learning comes from the connectionist camp. Two leading figures in the field of "parallel distributed processing," or PDP (a term used to described connectionist systems), David Rumelhart and James McClelland, claim to have developed a system that learns the past tense of English verbs. The following passage, by two critics of Rumelhart and McClelland, describes the venture.

> Using standard PDP mechanisms, this model learns to map representations of present tense forms of English verbs onto their past tense versions. It handles both regular (*walk/walked*) and irregular (*feel/felt*) verbs, productively yielding past forms for novel verbs not in its training set, and it distinguishes the variants of the past tense morpheme (*t* versus *d* versus *id*) conditioned by the final consonant of the verb (*walked* versus *jogged* versus *sweated*). Furthermore, in doing so it displays a number of behaviors reminiscent of children. It passes through stages of conservative acquisition of correct regular and irregular verbs (*walked, brought, hit*) followed by productive application of the regular rule and overregularization to irregular stems (e.g., *bringed, hitted*), followed by mastery of both regular and irregular verbs.[13]

I include this lengthy and somewhat technical passage to give the reader a feel for what research in connectionism is like, as well as to give an idea of what is at stake in the learning problem. The similarity between the way this system learns and the way a child learns points to another interesting aspect of artificial intelligence. Some researchers in cognitive psychology have viewed it as a valuable strategy for testing hypotheses about how learning takes place in human minds. The idea that the way the human mind works can be fruitfully studied by attempting to build computer simulations of it is called the "weak AI thesis" by the philosopher John Searle (The "strong AI thesis" is defined and discussed at length in Chapter 4.) This is another example of the interdisciplinary cross-fertilization of ideas and methods that AI research has stimulated.

So far, all of the AI projects that I have described have been academic

---

13.   Steven Pinker and A. Prince, "On Language and Connectionism: Analysis of a Parallel Distributed Processing Model of Language Acquisition," in *Connections and Symbols*, ed. Steven Pinker and Jacques Mehler (Cambridge, Mass.: MIT Press, 1988), p. 79.

projects: pure research in "toy" domains. But there have also been attempts to put artificial intelligence to work. The most notable examples of this fall under the heading of *expert systems*.

An expert system is a system that comprises a large database of useful information and a set of algorithms for using that information to make choices similar to those that a human expert would make. The idea is that an expert system uses a set of "heuristics"—principles of educated guessing—as opposed to sheer number crunching to arrive at its decisions. An early effort was the program DENDRAL, created by Edward Feigenbaum. DENDRAL had in its database a large amount of information about the molecular structure of known organic compounds. As input, it would accept data from mass spectrograph tests of an unknown substance. Using these data, its database, and heuristics, DENDRAL would attempt to figure out the identity of an unknown compound being analyzed. This is indeed a complex procedure, one that human experts find quite challenging. DENDRAL performed well.

Other expert systems have been developed for helping to locate oil deposits and aiding physicians in diagnosing illnesses. The challenging part in the development of an expert system is the creation and coding of the heuristics that the system will use. Typically, the developer will consult with human experts and attempt to copy the heuristics that they use. A difficulty is that human experts frequently do not *know* how they do what they do.

Expert systems are not generally created with an eye to penetrating any philosophical questions about the mind. Some people who do have a philosophical interest in artificial intelligence have declared them uninteresting for that reason. The reason for mentioning them in this book is that a few people have begun to consider the cultural risks of coming to rely increasingly upon expert systems instead of (if it is indeed instead of) human experts. I consider their arguments in the final chapter.

A seeming paradox of artificial intelligence is the fact that among the most daunting tasks for AI programmers are the things that humans and other animals accomplish with no effort at all. The recognition of faces and voices is a good example. The simulation of perception and recognition is an area of much recent work in artificial intelligence.

Although I will not undertake a thorough examination of it in this book, I should mention in passing that this is another area that appears, in the opinion of many researchers, well suited to connectionist strategies.

Thus ends the nickel tour. For those who would learn more, there is no shortage of books surveying the history and prospects of artificial intelligence from a generally nonphilosophical perspective.

This Book

In sketching the history of artificial intelligence, I have mentioned many of the problems and issues that are addressed later in the book. I did not mention one milestone that has a chapter all to itself. That was the appearance in 1950 of Alan Turing's paper "Computing Machinery and Intelligence."[14] Although I like to think that the *philosophy* of artificial intelligence began with the Poe essay discussed earlier, there is no question that Turing's paper marks the emergence of modern thinking on the subject. It is in this paper that what has come to be called the "Turing Test" was introduced. Almost immediately, it became a centerpiece of philosophical discussions of artificial intelligence, and remains so to this day.

Whatever one's views on the Turing Test may be, it is hard to deny that as a thought experiment it has transformed and sharpened our thinking about the mind and its relation to the rest of nature. So central is this thought experiment to the philosophy of artificial intelligence that it is fair to say that the central theme of this book is to explore this transformation and to consider some responses to it.

There are many possible approaches to writing about the philosophy of artificial intelligence. I have decided to begin with an overview of the classical themes in the philosophy of mind, and to call attention to them in considering the contemporary issues that are specific to AI. I also include a brief survey of the key concepts of symbolic logic, since those concepts are presupposed by all discussions of "formal" reasoning.

---

14. Originally published in *Mind* 59 (1950), 434-60; reprinted in *Minds and Machines*, ed. Alan Ross Anderson (Englewood Cliffs, N.J.: Prentice Hall, Inc., 1964), pp. 4-30. My page references will be to the larger volume.

Finally, I attempt to give a balanced presentation of the issues, but I make no pretense of neutrality. It is my view that an author gains nothing by trying to be invisible. Ideas are the property (and properties) of thinking beings, not just disembodied possibilities of belief. I am skeptical of many of the philosophically stronger claims coming out of AI research; I am one who suspects that the nature of the mind may remain mysterious for a long time yet. Nevertheless, my skepticism is not meant to be pessimistic. The sciences of the mind may be young, but the philosophy of mind can still learn much from them. If I can give to the reader a sense of the difficulty of this terrain and the excitement of trying to traverse it, I will consider my efforts successful.

Chapter 2

The Mind-Body Problem

Grasping the Problem

Human persons are creatures who, like all creatures, have a physical, biological nature. Our bodies are an important part of what we take to be essentially human about ourselves. We recognize and understand the capacities and limitations of our bodies, and we even measure the passage of time by our sense of growth and aging.

Already, though, language exerts a kind of centrifugal force upon thinking; it pulls away from complete *identification* with the body. We say, "I have a body," which implies that whatever I am, it is not quite the same thing as my body, since that which has cannot be exactly the same as what is had. This may appear to be a mere linguistic quirk, but it points to a much larger philosophical issue. That is, it points to the fact that it is very basic to our way of thinking about ourselves that we are not *just* bodies, not just creatures with a biological nature. Whether or not you share this intuition as a part of your personal philosophical system, there can be no doubt that it is embedded in the worldview of the West. How it got to be so embedded is a question that we shall take up later in this chapter.

Let's take a closer look. Consider the moment of waking up in the morning. Perhaps you have been dreaming, but the quality of your dream experience changes somehow. Some sounds that were in your dream now have the character of being external to your dream, and in fact the dream is now over. Your eyes flicker open to take in a complex of color and shape, which you understand without a moment's hesitation to be the real world. You are seeing and hearing, already engaged in interaction with the world. Moreover, your thinking is probably already detached from the specific sensory information being presented to you. You are thinking about whether to get up or lie there for a few more minutes, what to have for breakfast, what to wear, what to do today, and so on.

This detachment of your thinking from your perception—an obvious and constant fact of human experience—is very important. It marks a kind of cleavage of experience into two parallel streams. First, there is the stream of experience that you take to be the record of the world impinging upon you, the world of sight, sound, and feeling. Then there is the stream of experience that we usually refer to as "thinking." The literary term "stream of consciousness" is somewhat misleading, since it misses the cleavage that we have just noticed. Thinking and perception are both things that take place in the stream of consciousness, yet they are separate somehow.

Both streams are streams of *experience*; that much is very clear. Together, they appear to constitute the total of a person's experience while awake.[1] But these two streams are also clearly different. We need to consider what is different about them, and why we take them to be two streams instead of one in the first place.

First, there is the matter of control. You have very little control over the way things sound or look. To be sure, you can close your eyes or put your fingers in your ears, giving you an indirect kind of control, but you have almost no direct control over the exact character of your perceptions. On the other hand, your thinking does appear to be very much, though not absolutely, under your conscious control. You can decide what to think about, to some extent, and what not to think about. Of course, it is important not to overstate the extent of your sovereignty over your thinking. Try *not* thinking about monkeys for the next minute. Consider

---

1. This presupposes a fairly liberal understanding of perception and thinking, of course. There may be good reason later to narrow our understanding of these terms, but for now the point should be clear enough.

the number of times you have had a fragment of a song or an advertising jingle "stuck" in your thinking for the better part of a day.

Still, even the limited control that you have over your thinking is far more extensive than the control that you have over perception. This difference in control is therefore one intuitive basis for dividing the stream of experience into two streams. Now consider another aspect of this division. When you are with other people, you can talk about your *shared* perception of the world. That is, your perceptions are confirmed by other perceptions, in a certain way. If you see a tree, you can say to the person with you, "Do you see that tree?" If you *hear* the person say "Yes," then that is another perception of yours, which confirms the previous visual perception that you just had. Why do you take the second perception to be a confirmation of the first? It is because you believe that what you perceive to be another person is in fact another person like yourself who has the same kind of experiences. Your question, and that person's answer, mark what is taken to be the *public* character of the world. The world is out there for all to see, and that is why we expect to agree on such things, for the most part. This is sometimes referred to as "consensus reality."

When it comes to your own thoughts, the other stream of experience, things are quite different. You do not expect that some other person can confirm that you are thinking about lunch at this moment, or that the wine tastes good to you, or that you have a headache. When you ask, "Is it warm in here or is it me?" you are appealing to this same distinction between the two streams of experience. In short, your thoughts are the scenery of your "inner life," the private domain of your own mind.

It is interesting to note that we often use words of *containment* to talk about the mind. We speak of what is "in" the mind, the "inner life" as opposed to the "external world." We may say that these are just metaphors, figures of speech. Perhaps. If so, they have a powerful hold upon us, because it is hard *not* to think of the mind as a kind of sealed-off space, to which the rest of the world is somehow external. If these labels seem arbitrary, try for a moment to think of your mind as external, while the things around you are internal. Perhaps for a moment it is possible to achieve this perspective, but it requires (for me, at least) a powerful burst of imagination. Yet it seems so *natural* to divide the world the other way, into an inner mind and an external reality. In everyday speech, when we say that something is "all in your mind," we mean that it isn't real, not a part of consensus reality.

As I say, this division seems natural, even inevitable. But it is precisely this division that gives rise to the mind-body problem. After all, what we have been calling the external stream of experience is more simply understood as our awareness of objects in the external world. This includes not only the book in your hands but your hands themselves and the rest of your body. Your body is, after all, from one perspective just one more bit of the furniture of the external world. You can see it and others can see it; it is part of consensus reality. Even your brain, considered for the moment simply as part of your body is an object in the external world. It is not generally visible to the naked eye, but it can be made visible. During brain surgery a section of your skull may be removed, allowing you (with the aid of mirrors) and everyone else to see it. Your mind, in the sense of an inner stream of experiences, is something else again. Your intuitive sense of the matter is likely to be that your mind is not just that brain that you see in the mirrors, that the brain is *external* to your mind. How can both of these somehow be *you*? What is it about this particular body that makes it *your* body and not someone else's? How does your mind come to enjoy such an intimate and unique relation to your body? What is that relation?

Continuing to work from the level of intuition, some further observations can be made. For one thing, the body isn't just *there*; it clearly has effects on the mind. I have already mentioned perception as giving rise to one stream of experience. This process involves the direct participation of the body. It is light striking the retina of your eye, or sound waves upon your eardrum, that initiate the sequence of events that somehow cause (or become) your perceptual experiences. This is an example of events in your body causing events in your mind.

At other times you may think about what to do, then decide what to do, then do it. Here the sequence begins with events in your mind—thinking—which bring about events in your body—your voluntary behavior or action.

The simplest conclusion to draw, at first glance, is that at least some physical events can cause mental events and at least some mental events can cause physical events. There are definite limits, however. Although I may be able to bring about events in my own body by thinking, it seems that I cannot bring about events in someone else's body in the same way. Similarly, my smashing my toe against a rock cannot bring about your pain. The interaction between the mental and physical seems to be limited to a mind and one particular body. We can see that it is even further limited when we consider the fact that most of the events in my body do not give rise to any experiences at all. The beating of my heart is happening all the time that I am alive, but I do not normally *experience* it except during intense emotion or strenuous exercise. Likewise, my deliberation and deciding cannot bring about any event in my body that I might wish. Again, the beating of my heart is not the outcome of any thoughts and decisions on my part.[2]

To sum up, it is our intuitive sense that minds and bodies are quite different sorts of things that leads to what has come to be called the *mind-body problem*. I use the word "intuitive" here because at each step of the discussion I have had to make an appeal to intuition to sort things out. Note that "intuitive" does not mean "obvious"; it may take a good deal of reflection to come to see clearly what the mind-body problem is.

The mind-body problem is not by any means the only problem in the philosophy of mind, but it is central and tends to reappear in the examination of other problems. It is a sufficiently vexing problem that a number of attempts have been made to show that it is somehow based upon a confusion, or otherwise defective. If a problem can be shown to be defective, it doesn't have to be solved. Once it is clearly revealed as a pseudo-problem, it can be ignored. Therefore, determining whether the mind-body problem is a pseudo-problem is an important part of the problem itself.

---

2. There are unusual individuals who can exert a certain amount of voluntary control over the activity of their heart, but this only shows that the details of which physical events can be affected by which mental events is subject to considerable variation. Loss of muscle function by paralysis shows the same thing.

Classical Theories

Platonic Dualism

Plato is usually cited as the first Western philosopher to offer a theory of mind and body, even though he was not working from a sense of the mind-body problem as sketched above. In the dialogue called *Phaedo*, Plato (narrating the words of Socrates, his teacher) attempted to give an account of the possibility of the immortality of the soul. What Plato (and Socrates) meant by the soul was not quite the same as what that word has come to mean in religious contexts, nor is it the same as what we have been calling "mind" in the discussion above, but it is related to both of these.

Plato apparently believed that one of the soul's most important attributes is its capacity for abstract intellectual thought, while one of its least important attributes is its capacity for perception. In fact, Plato believed that what we have been calling the "external world"—the visible world of concrete objects and processes—is only part of reality, and by no means the most important part. In addition to the visible world there is, thought Plato, an "intelligible world" of abstract ideas and relationships that exist independently of the mind. What makes this notion philosophically interesting is the fact that Plato offered a fairly sophisticated argument in defense of it. It is worth taking the time to review that argument.

Imagine two metal rods, apparently of equal length. I say "apparently" because you will probably concede that if you were able to subject the rods to a sufficiently precise microscopic analysis, you would find that they are in fact not equal in length. If you think about it, you might also concede that no two rods are ever exactly equal in length.

That's fine, but Plato went on to ask how, then, we have any concept at all of what "exactly equal" might mean, if we never actually encounter it in the visible world. How could we know that a given pair of rods is closer to "exactly equal" than another pair, if exact equality is something that we have never experienced. Plato believed that since we do have a concept of exact equality it follows that we do have some experience of it, even though that experience could not be based in the visible world.

It is as an abstraction, an object of intellectual appraisal, that we understand what exact equality is; the objects of the visible world may approach it, but they never quite reach it.

So, in order to account for our understanding of certain facts about the visible world, such as the fact that no two objects are ever exactly equal in length, Plato had to suppose that there is another world, populated by objects of a different sort: abstract objects. He called these objects "forms." While the senses perceive the objects of the visible world, it is the mind (or soul) that "perceives" or apprehends the objects of the intelligible world.

Plato took the argument further. Although the objects of the visible world are subject to change, decay, and extinction, the objects of the intelligible world are eternal and unchanging. The concept of exact equality, for example, is what it is, regardless of the variation in visible objects. Since the human mind has a kind of access to this realm of eternal and unchanging ideas, it must itself be in that world. And since decay and death are phenomena of the visible world only, it follows that the part of a person that is of the intelligible world would not suffer these processes. Conclusion: the mind/soul is immortal, while the body is mortal.

There is not space to consider fully the details and problems of this argument. What is important about it is that it divides all of reality into two categories of being, with the mind in one category and the body in another. This move is called *dualism,* and this particular flavor of dualism is called, not surprisingly, *Platonic dualism.*

Cartesian Dualism

As I mentioned, Plato's dualism was not specifically a response to the mind-body problem; it was a response to other philosophical questions, such as the possibility of immortality and man's true nature. In fact, it would not be far wrong to say that our sense of mind and body posing a problem is a *result* of Plato's dualism, since it directs our attention to these issues in a focused way.

In the seventeenth century, the French polymath René Descartes articulated the mind-body problem in a more formal way, and it is Descartes's formulation that has come to serve as the basis for modern examinations of the problem. Descartes was also the first to appreciate the possibility of *automating* much (but not all) of human behavior, and is therefore one of the earliest figures in the philosophy of artificial intelligence.

Like Plato, Descartes was not specifically interested in the mind-body problem; he was working out a larger plan. The seventeenth century was a period of intense political and intellectual ferment. The Protestant Reformation had already occurred, and as a result the Roman Catholic church could no longer be viewed as the only possible source of legitimate opinions on important questions. Important scientific discoveries were being made that challenged the traditional theologically informed conception of man and his place in the universe. The "Copernican revolution," according to which mankind's place is not in the center of the universe, was not just a revolution in astronomy; it was a revolution in thought, dislodging a centuries-old picture of the world.

Descartes, like many intellectuals of this period, was concerned about the breaking up of the unified picture of the world that had been in place for so long. He himself made important contributions in science and mathematics and was as aware as anyone of the way in which human knowledge, while growing, was no longer held together in a coherent system. This need to see things as elements of a coherent system is perhaps the deepest expression of the philosophical impulse. What Descartes set out to do, then, was to find *foundations* for knowledge. That is, he hoped that he could show that all human knowledge, no matter how diverse and apparently unrelated, was in fact related by resting on a common set of foundations.

Foundational knowledge, if it could be shown to exist, would have to be the most basic possible knowledge and, since a structure is only as strong as its foundations, it would have to be as certain as possible. To this end, he devised what has come to be called the "method of doubt." The application of the method is fairly simple: For each thing that you might *claim* to know, ask whether it could conceivably, under any imaginable circumstances, be subject to doubt. If the answer is yes, then put that bit of alleged knowledge aside, as if it were false; it cannot serve as a foundation of all knowledge. Apply this method systematically and see what, if anything, does *not* get put aside. If anything survives the method of doubt, it will be an appropriate foundation of knowledge, since it is immune to doubt.

Consider the knowledge that you get by using your senses. You would claim to know, for example, that you have a book in your hands right now, and that knowledge-claim is based on a sensory experience you are having. Could this knowledge-claim be subject to doubt under any imaginable circumstances? Note that this is not the same as asking whether you do in fact doubt it at this very moment. Rather, the question is: *Could* you doubt it?

Of course you could. It is not hard to think of cases in which you are completely misled by your senses. To give a somewhat farfetched example, you might be hallucinating this book. Or you could be dreaming that you are reading a book. It doesn't matter that you don't for a moment believe that you are hallucinating or dreaming; what matters is that you concede that you *could* be. If so, you must reject sensory knowledge as foundational.

Perhaps, like Plato, you would turn to the realm of the pure intellect. You would claim to know that 2 + 2 = 4. Could you be mistaken in this sort of knowledge? It's hard to see how you could, but Descartes went so far as to suppose that there is some demon who deceives us whenever we set out to do any mathematical thinking. Again, the point is not that there is such a demon, but that there could be. If knowledge of the pure intellect, such as mathematical knowledge, is susceptible to error in this way, then it cannot serve as a foundation of all knowledge.

It seems that if Descartes is going to allow such wild possibilities as hallucination and demonic intervention to play a role, then nothing is truly immune to doubt. So it seems, but it is at precisely this point that Descartes introduces his most famous proposition: I think, therefore I am. That is, whatever else it may be possible for me to doubt, I cannot doubt my own existence. To do so would be to be thinking about my own existence, since doubting is a way of thinking, and if there is thinking going on there must be someone doing the thinking. The very act of doubting my own existence proves it beyond any possible doubt, argued Descartes.

I begin, then, with my own existence as a genuinely foundational piece of knowledge. Descartes went further, to reflect upon what sort of thing it is of whose existence I am now assured. When I conclude that I think, therefore I am, what is the very minimum that I am entitled to assert about the nature of this "I"? Since the existence of "I" is established by the fact of thinking, it would follow that the one thing I know about "I" is that it is a thinking thing. "I am a thing which thinks," wrote Descartes, dubbing this entity with its Latin name, *res cogitans*. I cannot doubt my own existence *as a thinking thing*. But I *can* doubt my own existence as a physical entity extended in space—*res extensa*. The only basis I have for concluding that my body exists is sensory, and sensory knowledge has already been shown by the method of doubt to be uncertain.

Now follows the key move, in relation to the mind-body problem. If my body is capable of being doubted but my mind is not capable of being doubted, then my mind has at least one property that my body lacks: immunity to doubt. Furthermore, this immunity to doubt was supposed by Descartes to be an *essential* property of the mind. That is, it is a property without which it could not even *be* a mind (as opposed to an "accidental" property, which a thing might or might not have). If mind and body do not have all the same essential properties, then they cannot be one and the same thing; they must be different things.

Once again, we end up with dualism. The world contains two (at least) kinds of things: thinking things and things extended in space, *res cogitans* and *res extensa*. Since mind is not extended in space, it cannot be said to have any specific location, but since thinking does have duration, it follows that mind is extended in time.

This form of dualism is called, appropriately, "Cartesian dualism." It is the form of dualism that has been most influential in modern discussions of the mind. It would be fair to say that Cartesian dualism has become the basis of the "common sense" understanding of the mind.

Descartes visited the Royal Gardens at Versailles and saw there the world-famous exhibit of automata. These were mechanical animal and human figures that turned and moved in what seemed at the time to be lifelike ways, driven by the hydraulic power of water pumped from the fountains. Descartes was impressed. He was so impressed, in fact, that he decided that the physical processes of the human and animal bodies must operate according to similar principles. The body, on this view, is a complex mechanical apparatus. He even described a hydraulic model of behavior. It was known that the brain contained fluid-filled cavities and that a clear fluid would drip from cut nerves. It was reasonable to propose that the muscles move the limbs by hydraulic power, with the reservoirs of hydraulic fluid in the brain.

Still, Descartes would not go so far as to suppose that *all* human experience could be reduced to mechanical-hydraulic principles. He asserted, for example, that no automaton of any complexity could learn to use language, that for that task a mind is required.

Although it may not seem so now, it was a bold stroke of imagination for Descartes to conceive of a biological organism as an automaton, and even bolder to conceive of the person as such an automaton linked somehow to an immaterial mind. It is only with this picture in place that modern discussions of the philosophy of mind and artificial intelligence make sense.

Recent Approaches

One of the most striking features of the worldview that emerged from the breakdown of the authority of the Church and the emergence of science was mechanism. Newton's laws of motion purported to describe not just the behavior of this or that object or system, but of any physical object or system at all. These laws involved a careful bookkeeping of forces, masses, momenta, and energy. Just as the behavior of a clock is driven by the energy stored in its wound mainspring, the behavior of any physical system should not exceed, in its expenditure of energy, the sum of energy available to it. Since clocks were complicated but well-understood devices, the metaphor of world-as-clockwork had a great appeal.

In more contemporary language, we say that energy is "conserved" in a closed system. A closed system is one in which no energy is allowed to enter or leave, so the conservation law says simply that, under those conditions, no energy will appear or disappear; the net amount of energy in the system will remain the same.

Now think of the human brain, and the entire human organism, as such a system. Whatever happens there must, according to the law of conservation of energy, be accounted for by energy available to the system. In this case, that energy is in the form of chemical energy derived from foods eaten. It is not at all clear what the role of an immaterial mind could be in this system. If, as Descartes supposed, the brain is the controller of a complex hydraulic system, then that system must be driven by physical energy. How could a mind, which has no mass or size or even location, exert any influence on a mechanical system? How could the "actions" of a mind make any difference at all?

This is the "problem of interaction," and Descartes himself was aware of it. His "solution" was to suppose that there is some physical region where the interaction takes place, an organ devoted to just that purpose. His candidate was the pineal gland, a small almond-shaped organ located on the center axis of the brain, three inches or so in back of the point between the eyebrows. Here, he thought, the mind could move the "animal spirits"—a hypothetical energylike fluid—which would in turn make the body work.

This is no solution at all, of course. For one thing, the problem of interaction is hardly solved by saying that the mind only interacts directly with a part of the brain, since it was not the size of the brain that was the problem. The problem is to show how a massless, sizeless, immaterial mind could have any effect at all on any physical system, large or small. If the mind is adding energy to the system somehow, then it ought to be possible in principle to detect that empirically.

In short, at the same time that Descartes was creating the common-sense picture of the mind, he was laying the groundwork for the eventual opposition to his theory. So successful was his image of the body as a mechanical device that it was not long before people began to wonder if the more problematic part of his model, the immaterial mind, was necessary at all. In 1749 the French physician and philosopher Julien

Offrey de la Mettrie published *L'Homme Machine* (Man the Machine), in which he promulgated a thoroughly mechanistic philosophy of the person, a view offensive to many of his contemporaries.

Materialism

The principal alternative to dualism is materialism. According to materialism, there are not two categories of things in the world but only one: material, or physical, things. Everything that happens in the universe involves physical objects, forces, and processes, and nothing stands outside of that totality of physical interactions. For all physical phenomena, physical causes must be sought and can, in principle at least, be found.

Materialism is the metaphysics of modern science, for the most part. That is, most working scientists are convinced that there is nothing in the world that is not subject to and ultimately explained by the laws of physics. It is important to recognize that although Descartes worked near the beginning of the scientific age, his dualism was almost a desperate last stand against the tide of materialism. Although dualism may remain basic to the common-sense picture of the mind, a wide gulf has opened between that common-sense picture and the scientific picture.

The twentieth-century philosopher Gilbert Ryle, in his book *The Concept of Mind,* lampooned the Cartesian conception of mind as a "ghost in the machine." What he meant was that the materialistic conception of the person is complete in itself; it is unnecessary to suppose that there is some additional entity called a "mind" to make the thing work. In fact, according to Ryle, to suppose that the mind must be some sort of "thing" or entity is to commit a "category mistake." A category mistake is the result of grouping something in a category with other things that are logically dissimilar. To use an example of Ryle's, if you visit a university and are shown the classroom, dorms, administration buildings, and so forth, and then ask, "But what about the university," you are making a category mistake. The university is not something in addition to its grounds, buildings, students, faculty, and the like; these things and people just *are* the university. On this view, the mind is not a substance or entity, immaterial or otherwise, that is somehow above or beyond the organic brain; it is an aspect or property of the physical organism.

It is important to recognize that Ryle—and materialism in general— is not claiming that minds do not exist. Rather, materialism claims something about what minds are. In fact, materialism is not a single well-defined claim at all; it comprises a number of variations, with important differences. Minimally, however, materialism says that nothing beyond what we understand to be the physical universe is involved in minds and mental processes.

Since materialism is actually a *class* of theories, it will be useful to sketch some of the more important variations.

The Identity Theory

According to this theory, minds and brains are identical or, alternatively, mental states are brain states. This is much stronger than claiming that mental states are *correlated* with brain states; a dualist would very likely agree with the latter claim. The identity theorist is claiming that mental states and brain states are one and the same. This claim implies that the terms "mental state" and "brain state" refer to exactly the same thing, just as "Peking" and "Beijing" refer to the same city.

Although the identity theory seems admirably clear and simple, there are some difficulties associated with it. To understand those difficulties, it will first be necessary to take a closer look at Descartes's position on dualism. Recall that Descartes's argument for dualism pivoted on the claim that mind and body cannot be one and the same if their essential properties are not the same. This claim is based on a principle that has come to be called the "indiscernibility of identicals." If A is identical to B, then all properties of A must be properties of B, and vice versa. Descartes argued that since the body is subject to doubt and the mind isn't, the two are not indiscernible, and hence not identical.

Descartes's argument has subsequently been criticized for the way in which it depends upon the beliefs of the person involved. To make this criticism clear, consider the following example: Is it possible that you could be certain that the Prime Minister of Britain is alive but doubt that John Major is alive? Yes, it is possible if you don't know that Mr. Major is the Prime Minister. Would it follow, from the fact that you can doubt that Mr. Major is alive, that he is not the Prime Minister? Obviously it wouldn't.

By similar reasoning, the fact that the body's existence—but not the mind's—can be doubted doesn't prove anything about whether the mind and body are identical. Does this invalidate the principle of indiscernibility of identicals? No, but it shows that the principle needs to be clarified a bit. For A and B to be identical, what is required is not that they should have *all* properties in common; we now know that that is too strong. Rather, A and B have to have all properties of a certain sort in common. The trick is to say just what sort of properties count in identity claims and what sort do not.

Intuitively, what we want are only those properties that do not depend upon what somebody *believes* about a thing, since what one might or might not manage to doubt clearly depends upon what one believes. The fact that somebody might doubt that Mr. Major is the Prime Minister doesn't tell us anything about whether he is or isn't the Prime Minister. Let's call those properties that a thing has that do not depend upon what anybody believes about it its *objective properties*.[3] Now we can restate the principle of indiscernibility of identicals as follows: A and B are identical if and only if every objective property of A is an objective property of B, and vice versa. If we then claim that being subject to doubt is not an objective property, Descartes's argument for dualism fails. This doesn't mean that dualism is false, of course, but only that Descartes's particular argument doesn't support it.

Getting back to the identity theory, the revised version of the principle of indiscernibility of identicals can be applied to the claim that

---

3. In technical philosophy, the matter is discussed not in terms of properties but in ᴜerms of predicates that truly apply. The particular kind of predicates that correspond to what we are calling "objective properties" are "extensional predicates." I mention this only because this technical language is fairly common in the literature on the subject, even though introducing it here would make matters unduly complicated.

mental states are identical with brain states. If even one objective property of mental states can be found that brain states lack, or vice versa, then the identity theory is certainly false.

One property that has been much discussed in this connection is *privileged access*. That is, I seem to have a kind of access to my own mental states that no one else can have. I know my mental states from the inside, as it were. In fact, when I first introduced the mind-body problem at the beginning of this chapter, I did so in terms of a division of experience into two streams. One stream is part of "consensus reality" while the other is not. I claimed as a basic intuition that I have a special access to this latter stream. That I have this access appears to be an objective fact about my mental states. My brain states, however, are publicly accessible, as was stated earlier; they are there for anybody to observe.

So, if I really do have privileged access to my mental states (and not my brain states) and if privileged access really is an objective property, then the identity theory is just wrong. Predictably, both suppositions have come under attack. Some philosophers have denied that there is any such thing as privileged access, while others have disputed whether any such thing could properly be called "objective."

You may wonder how anyone could challenge the claim that one has privileged access to one's own mind. The identity theorist may say that there is no reason in principle why someone's mental states could not be revealed by a microscopic inspection of his brain (assuming that we knew what to look for). If that is true, then there is nothing that that person could think that could not be discovered by someone else.

Still, you might argue, we couldn't come to know these things in the same way—that is, by introspection—that he knows them. True, but the identity theorist will respond that that is beside the point. If someone can determine (reliably) *what* another is thinking, then regardless of *how* it is done, the other's access is not privileged.

Another issue connected with the identity theory is the clarification of the actual terms of the identity equation. So far, I have been using the terms "mental state" and "brain state" as if it were intuitively obvious what these are. But there is an added distinction that is very relevant to the meaning of these terms: the distinction between *type* and *token*.

A type is simply a category of objects, whereas a token is a particular object. The word "apple," for example, refers to a type of fruit. When we say something like "this apple," we are usually referring to a token of that type—a particular apple. You can eat apple-tokens, but you can't eat apple-types (even though you can eat apples of different types).

The distinction is clear enough as it refers to apples, but is often forgotten when the subject is mental and brain states. Consider the mental state of believing that it will rain within an hour. It is possible that one might have such a belief many times, so it is reasonable to refer to the belief-that-it-will-rain-soon as a belief-type. On the other hand, it makes equal sense to think of it as a belief-token, if you think of the belief as a particular event that occurs at a particular moment in time. Clearly, belief-tokens are unique objects that occur but once, while belief-types may be "tokened" any number of times. Beliefs are mental states,[4] but the same type/token distinction applies to brain states.

It is one thing to say that every mental state–token is identical to some brain state–token. It is quite another thing to say that every mental state–type is identical to some brain state–type. Since tokens by definition never recur, the token-token identity theory asserts no more than that whenever a person is in some mental state, she is in some brain state or other, and that that mental state just *is* that brain state. Many versions of dualism would allow that every mental state is correlated with some brain state; it is the identity claim that the dualist feels goes too far. What the token-token identity theory does not allow is disembodied mental states, or minds without brains.

The type-type identity theory is much stronger. According to it, whenever a person is in a mental state of a particular type, she must also be in a brain state of some corresponding physical type, and to change mental state–types is to change brain state–types. As in the token-token version of the identity theory, the claim of correlation is strengthened by

---

4. Or events. The difference between a state and an event is that an event is a sequence of one or more states in time.

an identity claim: Mental states of a particular type just *are* brain states of a particular type. It should therefore be possible in principle to make lawlike claims of the form, "If A is in a mental state of type $M1$, then there must also be some identifiable type of brain state $B1$ that A is in." Furthermore, if it makes sense to say that two individuals, A and B, are ever in the same mental state, such as the state of believing that it will rain soon, then it must follow that their brains are in states of the same physical type.

But this is all very implausible. For one thing, what evidence is there that my brain is in the same state whenever I believe that it will rain soon? I could conceivably be in any number of brain states and have that belief. Worse, it is very unlikely that two people are ever in precisely the same brain state, if we take a brain state to be a specific pattern of activity and excitation of neurons. Perhaps the notion of "same state" needs to be relaxed somewhat. The problem is understanding just how to relax it. What we cannot do is say that two brain states are "the same" if they support (or embody, or are identical to) the same mental state. We cannot say this because it begs the very question at issue.

Carrying these objections further, it would seem to follow from either version of the identity theory that anything without a brain must also be without mental states. But what is a brain? It is a type of biological organ with a certain molecular and chemical structure. We can easily imagine being visited by intelligent extraterrestrials with organs that do the same kinds of things that our brains do but whose molecular and chemical structure is quite different. It seems that the identity theory would require that we deny that these beings could have any of the same mental states that we have. When the E.T. takes out an umbrella, we would have to say, "It's *as if* he believes it's about to rain."

You might want to change the definition of "brain" to make it looser on chemical and biological details but more explicit on functional ones. Perhaps a brain is "anything that controls a body." Such a move widens the field so much that it no longer deserves to be called a "mind-brain" *identity* theory.

It is also clear that it would be impossible in principle for computers to have mental states, since computers are not brains. If artificial intelligence involves any artificial mental states—and many supporters of artificial intelligence would insist that that is precisely what it involves—then according to the identity theory artificial intelligence is impossible. For the reasons given, such an approach seems unduly restrictive.

This is as far as I plan to go with this sketch of the identity theory. Many of the issues involved—especially the matter of privileged access—will surface again in later chapters. Since the identity theory is not the only version of materialism to be considered, it is important to consider some others.

Behaviorism

Ryle's "ghost in the machine" was an expression that perfectly captured the disdain that many scientists and philosophers had for "mentalism"—the attempt to place mental states and objects into a protected category. Dualism is perhaps the clearest expression of mentalism, but it is not the only expression of it.

To understand behaviorism as a reaction against mentalism, it is necessary to understand something of the philosophical and scientific movement called "logical positivism." This movement was—and in some ways continues to be—tremendously influential in shaping the scientific philosophy of the twentieth century.

Logical positivism was an attempt to bring philosophy into line with the tough-minded empirical methods that had proven so successful in the sciences, especially physics. It was widely accepted that that success was due to the rigorous application of the "scientific method," which involved, among other things, testing all hypotheses by observation and experimentation.

In the period between the two world wars, a group of scientists and philosophers had informal meetings in Vienna to discuss how philosophy and science might be somehow merged into a single intellectual endeavor. This group, which came to be known as the "Vienna Circle," comprised such individuals as A. J. Ayer, Moritz Schlick, and Rudolf Carnap. They recognized that before a proposition could reasonably be said to be true or false, it must be cognitively meaningful. "Cognitive" meaning is the sort of meaning that is relevant to the truth conditions of a proposition. Other, "noncognitive" varieties of meaning are possible, on this view, but not relevant to truth or falsity. If a proposition is not meaningful, it could not have truth conditions and therefore could not really be a proposition. The first problem, then, was to say precisely what it is for a proposition to be meaningful. If this could be accomplished, meaningful propositions could be distinguished from meaningless pseudo-propositions by applying an objective criterion. Science and scientific philosophy would, of course, restrict their attention to meaningful propositions.

First, it was noted that certain propositions are *formally* true. That is, their truth is a consequence of their meaning within some *formal system*. The concept of a formal system is the subject of the next chapter. For the moment, it is sufficient to say that a formal system comprises a set of symbols and precisely defined rules for manipulating them. The meaning of the symbols in the formal system is deliberately assigned, in an *interpretation*. The various computational techniques that we call "arithmetic" belong to a formal system. Thus, the proposition $7 + 5 = 12$ is perfectly meaningful and true in that formal system, or formally true. In that same formal system, $7 + 5 = 13$ is meaningful but false, and $= 7 + + 5$ is not even meaningful, hence neither true nor false.

The logical positivists proposed the Verification Principle for those propositions that do not derive their meaning from a formal system. Here is a simple formulation of the Verification Principle:

> A nonformal proposition is meaningful if and only if it is in principle verifiable by observation.

To "verify" a proposition in this context may be taken to mean "determine whether it is true or false." The words "in principle" are very important, since there are many propositions that are impossible *in practice* to verify, such as the proposition "There is intelligent life in the Andromeda galaxy." But as long as it is possible in principle to verify it by observation, the proposition is meaningful. The kind of observation that the positivists had in mind was *public* observation; that is, the verifying observation should be accessible to any observer, in principle.

You may be thinking that there was no need to make a special category for the formal propositions, since 7 + 5 = 12 is apparently verifiable by observing simple acts of counting. Although there are good reasons for doubting this,[5] a clearer example would be the following: The sum of every pair of odd numbers is an even number. Since this proposition applies to infinitely many cases, there is no question of verifying it by observation.

Now consider the proposition "Colorless green ideas sleep furiously." Is it meaningful? The Verification Principle says that for it to be meaningful, there must be circumstances under which one could *observe* it to be true or false. But it is hard to conceive of any such observation in this case. What would it be like to observe a colorless green idea furiously sleeping, or failing to? It seems safe to say that this proposition is not verifiable by any conceivable observation. So, according to the Verification Principle, it is quite meaningless and neither true nor false.

The application of the Verification Principle to these sample cases is clear enough. The logical positivists made a much more extensive and ruthless use of it. One philosopher, C. L. Stevenson, applied it to statements of moral judgment, such as "It is wrong to tell a lie." Since it does not seem possible to observe the wrongness of lying, Stevenson concluded that it is in fact not a meaningful proposition at all in the scientific or "cognitive" sense, but rather an expression of the utterer's emotional attitude toward lying, disguised as a proposition. So the statement has only noncognitive meaning. This positivistic theory about the meaning (or lack thereof) of moral language was called "emotivism." Similar moves were made for aesthetic judgments. If beauty is in the eye of the beholder, then its presence or absence is not publicly observable.

A domain of inquiry in which a rigorous application of the Verification Principle was apparently overdue was psychology. At first, J. B.

---

5. Not everything that you can count will follow the rules. Seven quarts of water plus five quarts of pure alcohol does not equal twelve quarts of solution.

Watson, the founder of psychological behaviorism, offered it as a methodological reform. How, he asked, can a science study such things as
ideas, beliefs, and desires if these things are not, in principle, observable? Psychology is supposed to be the science of the mind, but how can
there be such a science if it is impossible to formulate meaningful
propositions about the objects of the mind?

Consider belief. Beliefs are mental objects, most would agree. I may
see you leaving your house in the morning carrying an umbrella and
wearing a raincoat, and I may hear you say to me, "I think it's going to
rain today." I would certainly conclude that you believe that it will rain
today, but do I *observe* that belief? No. What I observe is what you wear,
what you carry, and what you say. I *infer* the belief from these observations, but I do not observe it.

Science should deal only in cognitively meaningful propositions,
which must be verifiable by observation. Beliefs, ideas, and other so-
called "mental objects" are not observable. Behavior is observable. The
conclusion is clear: The science of psychology should study behavior. This
argument became the foundation of *psychological behaviorism.*

In the form in which I have just stated it, psychological behaviorism
neither affirms nor denies the existence of the mind and mental objects;
it merely places the domain of scientific study elsewhere. And in fact it
brought about a great methodological revolution in psychology. A kind of
behavioristic orthodoxy grew up, with journals, psychology faculties,
and graduate students controlled by it. At the same time, behaviorism
was undergoing a kind of purification in the hands of philosophers.

Why stop with methodological recommendations? Why not go all the
way and claim that propositions that purport to refer to mental objects
either are meaningless or, at best, do not mean what people have usually
taken them to mean?

Positivism wanted to do for psychology what it had done for ethics.
The problem was that while emotivism said that statements in the form
of moral judgments were really expressions of the speaker's emotions, it
was not clear what statements about beliefs and ideas were really
expressing. The best solution was to propose that all mental terms really
refer to behavior or dispositions to behave, and that the mentalistic

language evolved simply as a shorthand. So, when I say that so-and-so believes it will rain today, what I really *mean* is that so-and-so is engaged in a certain kind of behavior (umbrella carrying, raincoat wearing, and the like) and nothing more.

If behavior is all that we really mean when we use mentalistic language, then you might wonder why it took so long for us to figure this out. The philosophical behaviorists used the analogy of sunrise and sunset. When people use the words "sunrise" and "sunset," all they are ever really referring to is the position and motion of the earth relative to the sun. They are not, and never have been, referring to the motion of the sun around the earth, because there is no such motion. The fact that for most of recorded history people didn't know what "sunrise" and "sunset" properly referred to doesn't alter these facts. Likewise, when we say "belief" we are referring to behavior, whether we acknowledge it or not.

This version of behaviorism has come to be called *philosophical behaviorism.*[6] From this vantage point, the whole mind-body problem is dismissed as a pseudo-problem, the result of a confusion about the real meaning of the language that we use. The word "mind" is just a convenient way of referring to a complex array of behaviors and dispositions, and the various other mental terms refer to subsections of that array and the relations between them. To assert that the mind is not the body is no more than to assert that the behavior is not the same as the thing that is doing the behaving, a harmless assertion. To suppose that the mind could exist independently of the body would be to suppose that there could be behavior in the absence of anything to do the behaving, a preposterous supposition. End of problem.

Philosophical behaviorism is classified under materialism because it is an essentially materialistic philosophy that gave rise to logical positivism in the first place, and ultimately to behaviorism. The material world is paradigmatically observable, and propositions about it are paradigmatically verifiable. It was the success of physics, after all, that provided the fuel for the positivistic movement. To a certain extent,

---

6. Or sometimes just "logical behaviorism."

logical positivism can be understood as the attempt to put the rest of human understanding in a position to imitate and partake of that success.

I have deliberately presented behaviorism as if its rise over the intellectual horizon were smooth and unimpeded. As you might expect, this was not at all the case. At every step of the way, logical positivism was challenged, as was behaviorism, from within and without. The Verification Principle itself was harshly criticized and subjected to endless amendments. While psychological behaviorism had smooth sailing for a while, since working psychologists were excited by the objective research program to which it pointed, philosophical behaviorism was embattled from the start. Still, philosophical behaviorism has left its mark on the mind-body problem. Indeed, it returns in a new guise in many discussions of artificial intelligence, as we shall see in the chapter that deals with the Turing Test.

Philosophical behaviorism faces a number of difficulties. For one thing, if a proposition is verifiable in principle by observation, the number of observations that count toward verifying it ought to be finite. Returning to the example of the person who has the belief that it will rain today, it is obvious that the statement "Joe believes it will rain today" cannot be translated into a statement about any *single* behavior. The number of behaviors that could be taken to "translate" this statement is quite large, arguably infinite. To have the belief that it will rain today is to be disposed to carry an umbrella *or* to wear a raincoat *or* to say "I think it will rain today" *or* to say "I believe it will rain today" *or* to wear galoshes *or*. . . . There seems to be no way to restrict the range of possible behaviors that are the meaning of this simple belief. The theory collapses under its own weight.

Functionalism

It has seemed to many philosophers that while philosophical behaviorism and the identity theory face serious difficulties, there is something right about both of them. The identity theory seems to be on the right track, if we could only get a less restrictive account of what a brain state—or a brain, for that matter—is. Behaviorism at least has the right sort of skepticism about mental objects, if we could only get a better account of what those objects actually are.

The theory that attempts to preserve what seems right about behaviorism without getting locked into the restrictions of the identity theory is *functionalism*. According to functionalism, mental states are just functional states of complex systems. To make sense of this simple claim, it is necessary to say in detail what a functional state is.

Let's begin with a simple example. Suppose that you and I have radio sets tuned to the same station. Your equipment comprises a modern solid-state tuner and amplifier, using integrated circuit technology. I have an antique radio that uses vacuum tubes and coils. There is a large difference in the quality of the sound produced by the two sets, but they are nevertheless producing the "same" music. Using a more general term, we may say that they are producing the same "output." They are also making use of the same input: the fluctuations in the surrounding electromagnetic field called "radio waves."

Since the input and output are the same, it follows that in some sense what both devices are doing with the input is the same: They are decoding it to produce music. But *how* they are doing it is rather different. So in one sense the two devices are doing the same thing; in another sense they are doing very different things. To understand these two senses, we need to introduce the idea of "levels of description" of a system.

This is actually a fairly complicated and subtle idea, but a simplified account of it should suffice to make the point about functionalism. Consider the two radio devices mentioned above. If we confine ourselves to a physical description of what they are and what they are doing, it is clear that they don't have much in common. They are made of different materials, and those materials are configured as parts in very different ways, and the physical interactions between those parts is also very different. At a higher level, however, we might just look at various parts of the system and describe them in terms of what they do. This part detects the radio signal; this part amplifies it; this part works the speakers. At that level of description, there is a correspondence between what the two devices are doing. And we have already granted that at the level of producing output they are doing just the same thing (though not equally well). We may call the higher level of description the "functional level," since it has to do with how a thing functions, rather than what it is made of.

We may further say that any device that detects radio waves and decodes them to produce audible music is *functionally equivalent* to any other device that does the same thing. Two systems are in functionally equivalent states if they can accept the same input and "process" it somehow to produce the same output.

Now imagine a third device, somewhat unusual in construction. This one is capable of detecting and decoding radio waves, but it is not able to send an amplified signal to the speakers. It does have a built-in cassette player, however, that can drive the speakers and produce audible music. Suppose that the music recorded on the cassette were exactly the same music that happened to be being played by the other two radio devices. So, while those two devices are playing broadcast music, this third device is playing a cassette recording of the very same music that is being broadcast. Is this third device functionally equivalent to the other two?

It is not. Even though it detects the same radio waves and is playing the same music as the other two, it is clear that there is not a *causal link* between the detection of the waves and the production of that music—it just happens that the inputs and outputs of all three devices are, for the time being, the same. What is different is the relation between input and output; the character of that input is not the *cause* of the specific character of the output.

Now consider how these concepts relate to the mind-body problem. According to functionalism, to be in a particular mental state is just for your brain (or central nervous system) to be in a particular functional state. If another brain is in that functional state as well, then it too is in that mental state. Furthermore—and here is the improvement on the identity theory—if something other than a brain, such as a digital computer, is in the same functional state, then it must also be said to be in the same mental state.

Functionalism is indifferent to what sort of system is producing the functional states, as long as it is sufficiently complex to produce them at all.[7] This is an important part of its appeal from the standpoint of developing a philosophy of mind that can accommodate the possibility of artificial intelligence (and extraterrestrial intelligence).

Note that this is not simply a disguised version of behaviorism. Mental states are not, according to functionalism, just output or dispositions to produce certain output. Rather, to be in a given mental state is to be processing input in a certain way to produce certain output. Consider the range of states that we call "mental": beliefs, ideas, hopes, fears, desires, and so forth. Functionalism says that when a being—or system—is "in" any of these states, it must also be in some particular functional state, and that there is a "type-type" correspondence between mental and functional states. Functional states are identified by the causal relations that they bear to each other and to inputs and outputs. Perhaps you see an apple, which reminds you of the color of your red sweater, which in turn reminds you that you must pick that sweater up at the dry cleaner's, which gets you to pick up the telephone to check to see if the sweater is ready. This is a long causally linked chain of mental states: a perception, a memory, another memory, a decision, and a volition.[8] If functionalism is true, each of these states is really just a functional state of your brain, causally linked in an analogous way. If we could get some other system to go through the same sequence of functional states, then we would have to attribute the same mental states to it.

It may be useful to attempt a slightly more formal definition of functionally equivalent systems.

> A state, $S1$, of system A is functionally equivalent to state $S2$ of system B if and only if A and B will reliably produce the same subsequent state and/or output, given the same input.

This causal isomorphism between mental and functional states implies that the two kinds of states will be individuated in the same

---

7. A doughnut, for example, just doesn't have the right sort of complexity to produce the functional states that your brain can produce.

8. That, of course, is just one way of describing the sequence.

way. Where one mental state ends and another one begins must also be where one functional state ends and another one begins. This requirement is, as we shall see later, a point on which functionalism has been widely criticized. Without it, however, there is no chance of revealing any sort of regular mapping between mental and functional states. Without such a mapping, it would be impossible to say that anyone who is in mental state M must also be in functional state F. And if we can't say that much, it is hard to see that functionalism has any very interesting content at all. The condition that A and B will *reliably* produce the same subsequent state or output is there to eliminate systems that just happen to do so.

At the moment, however, functionalism remains the favorite theory of the mind among artificial-intelligence advocates. Rather than enumerating criticisms here, therefore, I shall take them up as they are relevant to issues in later sections. It is also important to keep in mind that, strictly speaking, functionalism is neutral on the issue of materialism versus dualism. The functionalist has no official position on what a system must be made of to have functional states. If a Cartesian immaterial mind can have them, then that is what matters. This neutrality is somewhat disingenuous, of course; it is simply a way of sidestepping the ontological issues involved. It will come as no surprise to learn that most functionalists are staunch materialists who believe that only physical systems can have functional—and therefore mental—states.

Chapter 3

Computing Machines

At this point, we need to have a clearer understanding of what we are talking about when we talk about computers. The word "computer" connotes various things to different people. To some of us, it just refers to the little box-and-screen sitting on our desk, which we use for various kinds of work. Others may imagine big boxes with panels of flashing lights in air-conditioned rooms. Still others may not picture anything at all, but simply think of things that computers have brought to the world, such as cosmic errors in the gas bill, annoying phone calls, and automated dating services. Like television, computers are sufficiently a part of the cultural scene that we do not think much about what they are or how they do what they do; we think about how they make a difference in our lives. Sometimes, a way to think about this is to consider the effect that removing computers from society would have. The newest generation of bank account-holders may find it inconceivable that banking was done until fairly recently without the assistance of automated teller machines, a technology that is completely computer-dependent.

This level of understanding may suffice for coping in an increasingly computer-dependent society[1] but it won't do for giving a careful consideration to the philosophical issues occasioned by the computer revolution. If we are going to think about artificial intelligence as it relates to

---

1. And then again, it may *not* suffice. In the last chapter, we shall look at some of the human consequences of having a not-very-clear understanding of what computers are.

such questions as the mind-body problem, a deeper understanding is needed. This understanding is not possible without also grasping some slightly technical concepts and symbolism. The first such concept is that of a *formal system*.

Formal Systems

The most familiar examples of formal systems are certain kinds of games. As a simple example, let's look at the card game Solitaire,[2] which exemplifies many of the properties of formal systems.

To begin with, there is a stock of objects or tokens: a deck of cards. Each token has two properties that matter in this particular game—rank, color and suit—and these properties are unambiguously identifiable. As you turn cards over, there are also rules for combining them into "strings" of cards. Each card put down must be succeeded by a card of different color that is one less in rank. Anything else is not a legal string of cards. There are also rules for manipulating those strings, connecting and disconnecting them. The rules are unambiguous and exhaustive. That is, they "cover" every possible situation and provide an absolute way to determine whether a given card placement is legal or illegal; there are no "borderline cases."

Because it is a game, Solitaire has other aspects as well, such as a goal. That need not concern us here. It is possible to "play" Solitaire according to the rules of the formal system without trying to win.

To sum up, this formal system comprises:

1. A set of unambiguously identifiable tokens.

2. Combination rules for connecting tokens to form larger objects.

3. Rules for manipulating those larger objects.

In fact, the second and third rules may be thought of as a single kind

---

2.   There are several versions of this game. I am thinking of the one in which the player attempts to move cards to arrays of descending rank and alternating color and then transfers them to stacks in ascending rank by suit.

of rule, applied to different-sized objects in the formal system. There may be many levels of objects in a formal system, just as there are letters, words, sentences, and paragraphs in written English.

A more suitable example of a formal system is the arithmetic that we all learned in elementary school. First there is the set of tokens. This set comprises the digits 0, 1, 2, 3, 4, 5, 6, 7, 8, and 9, and the symbols +, -, ÷, ×, and =.[3] You also learned rules for combining these tokens into strings, such as 2 + 2 = 4 (but not 2 + = 24).

But wait! You didn't learn rules for manipulating strings and tokens; you learned rules for adding, subtracting, multiplying, and dividing *numbers*. Indeed, that is what you learned, but this brings up an important point about formal systems: until you *interpret* the tokens—assign a meaning to them—they are just arbitrary shapes or objects. They might be marks on a piece of paper, or chalk streaks on a black-board, or sticks of varying length. One of the key features of a formal system is just that *the rules for identifying, combining, and manipulating tokens do not have to make any reference to any meanings assigned to them.* In fact, this is precisely what makes it a "formal" system: all the moves can be made by someone who only knows the *form* of the objects involved, and nothing of their *meaning*. This is also why I talk about "token manipulation" instead of the more familiar "symbol manipulation." To call a token a symbol is already to indicate that it bears some meaning or is subject to an interpretation. That tokens can be used as symbols by people is irrelevant to their purely formal properties.

The fact is, you didn't learn arithmetic as a purely formal system. But you could have, even though it would be tedious, impractical, and pointless to do so. You could have been taught rules for fiddling with tokens on a page without ever being taught what the tokens stand for, and you would be able to "do arithmetic" as well as one who knows what they stand for. It is probably not stretching the truth to say that some of us, when it came to "higher" mathematics such as algebra and trigonom-

---

3. Actually, you probably used other symbols, such as a wide line to separate a column of added numbers from their sum, and a long-division symbol, but there is no need to clutter up the explanation to that extent. You *could* have used just the ones given here.

etry, *did* learn only the formal system aspect. How many of us, for example, were able to recite dutifully the Quadratic Equation and "solve for *y*" without having any real clue to what it all meant? For us, the "word problems" were our downfall, because our knowledge of the formal system far outstripped our knowledge of the interpretation, the concepts represented by the manipulations.

All of the purely formal rules of token manipulation are collectively referred to as the *syntax* of the system. Things such as meaning, truth, and falsity are components of the *semantics* of the system. Thus, considered simply as a string of tokens, 2 + 2 = 5 is well-formed; it doesn't violate any syntactic rules. Considered as a meaningful proposition, it is false.

There are many formal systems. One of them, however, is of special interest because it has been widely believed to capture the essence of rational thought. This system is called *logic*. As it is realized in a formal system, it is called *formal logic*. Although this chapter cannot take the place of a sustained study of logic, the concepts and language of logic are so deeply embedded in the artificial-intelligence research program that it is necessary to have at least a passing familiarity with this particular formal system.

Logic and Rationality

Man is a rational animal, according to Aristotle. That is, Aristotle saw rationality as one of the defining conditions of personhood. Many people regard rationality and intelligence as nearly synonymous, although we shall attempt some careful distinctions in a later chapter. Nevertheless, rationality is not the easiest concept to pin down. After all, nonhuman animals do things that we as observers would say are rational. And they learn things, a process that we also associate with rationality. Yet it is clear that this is not the whole story. Aristotle certainly did not mean that what is unique about man is the ability to do rational things and to learn, because these are *not* uniquely human properties.

Consider the matter more closely. When we say that it is rational for a bird to build its nest up off the ground, we do not mean that this behavior is the outcome of a process of reasoning. It is instinctive behavior. To call nest-building rational in this sense is simply to note that it is what a "rational agent" would do under the circumstances. The bird behaves as if it were a rational agent, even though it is not.

The aspect of rationality, then, that interested Aristotle was not the behavior but the thought processes that underlie it. These are evidently what make us "rational agents."

"Thought" is a vague word. Virtually anything that goes on in your mind can be called a form of thought: believing, hoping, considering, and so on. One of the thought processes that is most interesting in connection with rationality is the one called "concluding." Concluding is at least sometimes the outcome of considering. It involves trying to extract information from other information. To take an example, suppose that your car won't start. You turn the key in the ignition, and nothing at all happens. You wonder if the battery is dead. So you pull the headlight switch and the headlights come on, full and bright. You conclude that a dead battery is not the cause of your troubles.

The information with which you started comprises the simple facts that the car won't start and the headlights work. Your conclusion is a new piece of information—the battery isn't dead—which you extracted from that starting information.

As you are well aware, you can't conclude just anything from any-thing. To put it another way, not just anything "follows from" anything. The business of concluding—or "drawing conclusions," as we sometimes say—is governed by rules. Those rules are the subject matter of logic, just as the rules governing the manipulations of quantities are the subject matter of mathematics. Logic is about what you can (and can't) conclude from what, and what follows (and doesn't follow) from what.

The first thing to consider is what *kinds* of things are controlled by the rules of logic. It makes no sense, after all, to ask what follows from, say, a chair. No, the appropriate objects that are connected by logical relations are *propositions*. Although it is generally convenient to think of propositions as sentences, many philosophers make a distinction between the two. Consider the following three sentences:

Il pleut.
It's raining.
Es regnet.

There is no question that we have *three* sentences here, in French, English, and German. And they are, of course, *different* sentences. What they have in common is this: they represent the same proposition. Three sentences—one proposition. An interesting consequence of this is that the one proposition represented by all four sentences is not in any particular language. Sentences are in this or that language; propositions are not. Keep in mind that even though we shall talk mostly about this or that sentence, we are really interested in the propositions that are represented by those sentences.[4]

When you conclude a proposition from some other propositions, it is fair to call those other propositions the *reasons* for your conclusion. So another way to define logic would be this: logic is the study of how to get conclusions from reasons. In logic, "reasons" are generally called *premises*. Premises are any propositions offered as reasons for a conclusion. Premises and conclusion considered together are called an *argument*. Logic describes the rules of arguments.

Propositions have structure. That is, "It's raining and I'm wet" is clearly a more complicated proposition than "It's raining." Indeed, the latter proposition is contained in the former. In fact, you could consider the first proposition to be two propositions hooked together by the word "and." Thus, "and" acts as a "structure-word," a word that allows you to make longer propositions from shorter ones. Structure-words such as "and" are called *logical connectives*, for obvious reasons.

There are many logical connectives, but for now let's just focus on "and." Some additional important concepts have to be introduced. The first one is *truth-conditions*. Propositions have truth conditions, which are simply the conditions under which they are true or false. The

---

4.   It is a matter of some philosophic controversy whether there are any such things as propositions or, if there are, what sort of things they could be. There is no good reason to explore that controversy in this context. It is, however, relevant to questions about the mental *representation* of ideas.

truth-conditions for "It's raining" and "I'm wet" are obvious enough. Whether "It's raining" is true or false depends not upon logic but upon the weather. Logic can't tell you if or when a proposition is true or false, except under certain tightly defined conditions, which we'll get to later.

The proposition "It's raining and I'm wet" clearly depends, for its truth-value, upon the truth-values of the two propositions contained within it. If even one of them is false, the whole thing is false. If a proposition contains other propositions, linked by means of connectives, we say that it is *compound*. If it has no connectives and is therefore not compound, it is called *atomic*. Logic can't give you the truth-values of atomic propositions, but it enables you to determine the truth-values of compound propositions, given the truth-values of its component atomic propositions. Checking the weather tells you, say, that "It's raining" is false. Given that, logic tells you that "It's raining and I'm wet" is false.

If you think about it, you will realize that "and" affects the truth-conditions of all compound propositions in which it occurs in just the same way. If you have a proposition of the form "A *and* B," where A and B are any two propositions, it will be true if and only if the propositions A and B are *both* true; otherwise, it is false. A compact way to represent this information is in the form of a *truth-table*. A truth-table allows you to glimpse the truth-conditions of a proposition. Here's the truth-table for any and-proposition, henceforth to be called a *conjunction*. We'll use a special symbol, the $\land$, to represent the logical "and."

A	B	$A \land B$
T	T	T
F	T	F
T	F	F
F	F	F

Note that the two left-hand columns give you all the different possibilities of truth and falsity for A and B. Another way to think of it is this: each horizontal row of T's and F's represents the different ways that the world might be that have any bearing on the truth-value of "A and B." So, the third row tells you that in a world in which A is true but B is false,

"A and B" is false. Remember, the truth table represents how A and B *could* be; it does not tell you whether they are, in fact, true or false. And it tells you how the proposition "A and B" would be affected by the truth or falsity of A and B.

Consider the proposition "It's not raining." This, too, is a compound proposition, since it is formed by denying another proposition, namely the atomic proposition "It is raining." In logic, this is called *negation* and it is considered to be another connective, even though it does not join two other propositions. The important thing is that it is used to build compound propositions. Note that there are many ways in English (or other languages) to express this logical idea: "It's not raining ," "It is not the case that it is raining," and even "It rains not." We're looking at *logical* structure, not sentence structure.

Obviously, a negated proposition is true if and only if the unnegated proposition is false. This can be represented in a very simple truth-table. Again, a special symbol, the ~, will be used to represent this connective.

A	$\sim A$
T	F
F	T

We only need two rows in this truth-table, since there is only one sentence involved and therefore only two ways that the world could be that would affect the truth-value of "not-A."

There are many logical connectives, but logicians have selected a small group to work with. These represent structures that closely resemble those that are used in everyday language, although in logic they are precisely defined. For example, *disjunctions* are or-propositions. It happens that in English there are two ways of using the word "or." Sometimes it allows for both possibilities to obtain; sometimes it allows exactly one possibility to obtain. If your friend tells you that she wants a book or a tape for her birthday, you certainly would not conclude that she doesn't want both. In this case, you are interpreting the word "or" in its "inclusive" sense. On the other hand, if you tell the waiter that you'll take either butter or margarine on your baked potato, he will understand that you don't want both. He is interpreting the word "or" in its "exclusive" sense. The standard logical symbol for disjunction (the or-relation) is ∨.

The inclusive and exclusive senses of the English word "or" correspond to quite different logical connectives, with different truth-tables. Here they are:

A	*B*	*A* ∨ *B*
T	*T*	*T*
F	*T*	*T*
T	*F*	*T*
F	*F*	*F*

That was the truth-table, then, for the *inclusive disjunction.*

A	*B*	*A* ∪ *B*
T	*T*	*F*
F	*T*	*T*
T	*F*	*T*
F	*F*	*F*

That was the truth-table for the *exclusive disjunction.* I used an arbitrary symbol, the ∪, to distinguish it from the inclusive disjunction. As you can see, the truth-conditions differ in the case where A and B happen both to be true. Generally, when logicians use "or" they mean the inclusive disjunction.

An important connective is called the *material conditional,* or "if-then" structure. "If today is Tuesday, then this is Belgium." Again, this connective links two propositions to form a longer proposition. The "if" proposition in a material conditional is called the *antecedent,* while the "then" part is called the *consequent.* Note that in English these may occur in any order, without affecting the logical structure at all. "This is Belgium, if today is Tuesday." This sentence represents the same proposition as the preceding one, even though the consequent is stated first, and without the word "then." The logical symbol for the material conditional is →.

To understand the truth-conditions for material conditionals, consider first under what conditions the proposition would definitely be falsified. The proposition in the above paragraph would clearly be false if today were Tuesday and this were *not* Belgium. More formally, we can say that a material conditional is false if its antecedent is true and its consequent is false. As far as logic is concerned, that is the *only* time it is false; in all other cases it is considered true. Some people find this surprising. If you are one of these people, you should understand that the underlying principle is that a proposition is not called false unless it is explicitly falsified, and this is the only case in which a material conditional is explicitly falsified.

With this information in hand, the truth-table for the material conditional is fairly straightforward.

A	B	$A \to B$
T	T	T
F	T	T
T	F	F
F	F	T

In presenting the truth-tables for the two senses of "or," I mentioned that the difference in logical meaning is reflected in the different truth-tables. By the same token, truth-tables allow us to determine whether two propositions are logically *equivalent*— that is, whether they have the same truth-conditions. Consider the propositions "If he's not drunk then he's crazy" and "Either he's drunk or he's crazy."

D	C	$(\sim D \to C)$	$(D \vee C)$
T	T	T	T
F	T	T	T
T	F	T	T
F	F	F	F

The two propositions are shown to have the same truth-conditions and therefore are logically equivalent.

In fact, truth-tables can be used to test for a number of logical properties, but the central one that we started out with was this idea of propositions "following from" other propositions. It's time to apply these techniques to that.

If a conclusion follows from some premises, those premises are said to *entail* that conclusion. An argument in which the premises entail the conclusion is called *valid*. The definition of validity is this: An argument is valid if, and only if, it is impossible for all of its premises to be true and its conclusion false. That is, if the premises (of a valid argument) are true, then the conclusion must also be true. Notice that we do not say that the premises of a valid argument are or must be true. We merely say that *if* they were true, there would be no way for the conclusion to be false.

Consider the following argument: If today is Tuesday, then this is Belgium. This isn't Belgium. Therefore, today isn't Tuesday. In symbolic notation, the argument looks like this:

$T \rightarrow B$ ~ B therefore ~T

Is it valid? A truth-table provides the information that we need to decide whether it is valid:

T	B	$(T \rightarrow B)$	~B	~T
T	T	T	F	F
F	T	T	F	T
T	F	F	T	F
F	F	T	T	T

We want to know if the premises could all be true while the conclusion is nevertheless false. If so, the argument is invalid. So we look for a case in which both premises (*not* the atomic propositions) are true and the conclusion is false. Well, there is only one case (the fourth row) where both premises are true, and in that case the conclusion is also true. So it appears that there is no way for the premises to be true but the conclusion false—since each horizontal row represents a "way" the world might be—and the argument is therefore valid.

Entailment and validity are the central ideas of deductive logic. (There is also inductive logic, but that is another story.) They represent the correctness of the information that you extract from other information, the legitimacy of your conclusions. Truth-tables provide us with a precise, unambiguous way to say what it is for a proposition to follow from some other propositions.

All of the concepts have been presented to you in terms of their full intuitive meaning, so to speak. That is, we have talked in terms of propositions, and truth and falsity, and entailment. This is the semantic side of logic. The word "semantic" indicates that we are considering the meaning of the symbols that we are using. Truth and falsity are semantic notions because nothing can be true or false that is not first meaningful. As you already know, the other aspect of a formal system—the part that *makes* it a formal system—is its formal syntax. Consider the process of constructing truth-tables. It would be easy enough to give purely me-chanical rules for this, or to program a computer to do it. Filling in those T's and F's requires no special insight. In fact, I could have shown you how to do truth-tables without ever telling you what they mean, by simply giving you the rules for where to write T's and where to write F's.

To sum up, if you think about the formal system simply as symbols that you can manipulate according to mechanical rules, you are thinking about the *syntax* of the system. If you think about what it all means, you are thinking about the *semantics* of the system. Sentences, for example, are syntactic entities; propositions are semantic entities. Truth and falsity are semantic concepts; they depend upon meaning. Entailment and validity are likewise semantic concepts. If you glance back to the definitions of those terms, you'll see that they pertain to the truth and falsity of premises and conclusions. There is, however, a purely syntactic sense of "following from" that can be defined in terms of what symbol strings you are allowed to extract or derive from others.

What we gain by making this distinction between syntax and semantics is this: The syntax of a formal system is just the sort of thing that we can get a computer to work with. Therefore, we can program a computer to "do" logic, in some sense. To put a computer in touch with the semantics of a formal system is something else again. Doing so requires that the computer *understand* the strings that it manipulates. This question is addressed directly in the next chapter. We started out with the idea that rationality involves rules. The nineteenth-century logician George Boole characterized the principles of logic as the "laws of thought." We now see that some of those rules—the syntactic ones—can be "understood" (a semantic term, hence the scare quotes) by a digital computer. We are left with the philosophical problem of determining how much of rationality and intelligence is simply a matter of syntactic competence and how much (if any) is essentially semantic.

One sometimes hears the claim that a computer—any computer—is a "logical" machine. There is a sense in which this claim is correct and a sense in which it is wrong. A computer follows the instructions in its program. Given a knowledge of that program and the inputs, one can in principle predict exactly the output. In this sense the computer is no more logical than any other deterministic, nonchaotic system.

I showed how truth-tables can be constructed for compound propositions, and pointed out how the procedure for constructing them is purely mechanical. Does this mean that a computer could do it? If the machine is programmed to accept as input "sentences" that are already in the symbolic notation of the formal system, then programming it to construct truth-tables is not difficult. It is an open question whether we shall ever be able to program a machine to accept sentence strings in English or some other natural language, translate them into symbolic notation, and then construct the truth-tables. To do this, the machine would need to be able to deal with the semantics of a natural language.

At the level of circuitry, most digital computers *are* logic machines. The silicon chips are equipped with networks of *logic gates* that manipulate voltages according to the principles exhibited in truth-tables. If we designate one voltage level as 0 and the other as 1, the AND gate produces an output of 1 if and only if both inputs are 1. An OR gate lets the current flow if and only if at least one input is 1. Gates can be hooked together in manners structurally isomorphic to compound propositions as complex as you like.

None of these considerations prevent computers from being programmed to behave illogically, but the illogical behavior is at a higher level of description; at the level of circuits, the logic remains impeccable. In any case, the connection between what might be called "logical" behavior and *rational* behavior remains to be examined.

The reason for including this short survey of formal logic was to introduce some of the concepts that are most basic to our understanding of rationality into the discussion. You may be wondering how your own rationality is linked to the formal system of symbolic logic. You may also be wondering if artificial rationality is simply a matter of programming a digital computer to "do" formal logic (i.e., to test for properties such as equivalence and entailment). If you are unfamiliar with formal logic, you nevertheless probably do not believe that your rationality is compromised by that fact.

Rationality is a richer concept than "logicality" because it is linked to action. We call agents rational because they make rational choices, and choices can only be rational (or irrational) in light of the agent's desires, interests, and values. Furthermore, rationality has to work in a universe of imperfect and probabilistic information. Thus, making a rational choice involves more than enumerating the facts that one knows and extracting the deductively entailed consequences of those facts.

It is not so easy to spell out the conditions under which a choice is rational, and there is a large literature on the subject. The matter is of interest to AI researchers because they must grapple with understanding human rationality as a first step toward implementing artifical rationality.

A standard approach is called the "subjective expected utility" (SEU) theory. On this view, an agent has a set of desires which are ranked in importance. At a given occasion of choosing an action, the agent assigns to each possible action a probability that the result will be satisfaction of a desire. Thus, the agent calculates the "expected utility" of the various available courses of action. It is called "subjective" expected utility because it is based on the agent's subjective desires and available information. The idea is that once the agent has assigned a subjective expected utility to each possible action, she then employs a logical calculus of some sort[5] to arrive at the rational choice.

As straightforward as this sounds, there are some who claim that the SEU theory is not an adequate model of human rationality. If we are seeking to model artificial rationality upon human rationality, therefore, we will need a better model. Herbert A. Simon, a philosopher who is also an important figure in the AI movement, writes:

> The SEU model assumes that the decision maker contemplates, in one comprehensive view, everything that lies before him. He understands the range of alternative choices open to him, not only at the moment but over the whole panorama of the future. He understands the consequences of each of the available choice strategies, at least up to the point of being able to assign a joint probability distribution to future states of the world. He has reconciled or balanced all his conflicting partial values and synthesized them into a single utility function that orders, by his preference for them, all these future states of the world.[6]

After commenting on how much is never explained or just taken for granted in this model, Simon remarks,

> When these assumptions are stated explicitly, it becomes obvious that SEU theory has never been applied, and never can be applied— with or without the largest computers—in the real world.[7]

Simon favors a model that he calls "bounded rationality." It is a more modest model in that it supposes that rational agents have evolved to

---

5.   This would have to be a complex system involving both deductive elements, such as what was surveyed in this chapter, and inductive, or probabilistic, elements.

6.   Herbert A. Simon, "Alternative Visions of Rationality," *Reason in Human Affairs* (Stanford, Cal.: Stanford University Press, 1983); reprinted in *Rationality and Action*, ed. Paul K. Moser (New York: Cambridge University Press, 1990), p. 195.

7.   Ibid., p. 195.

handle single problems at a time, without paying too much attention to the connections between them. Our survival has not depended upon our having a "global utility function" that compares and ranks all of our various desires and values, so we don't have one. He says,

> In actual fact, the environment in which we live, in which all creatures live, is an environment that is nearly factorable into separate problems. Sometimes you're hungry, sometimes you're sleepy, sometimes you're cold. Fortunately, you're not often all three at the same time.[8]

To put it another way, the sort of rationality with which humans have been endowed by evolution is one that tends to pay attention to the details of immediate problems in preference to the larger linkages between them. It is therefore entirely possible that an individual will rely on a set of values and beliefs in one problem context and rely on an entirely incompatible set in another context. Consistency—one of the most crucial concepts in formal logic—is not so crucial to human rationality, if Simon is right.

Simon even conjectures that the purpose of emotions is to focus one's attention upon the problem at hand, which would tend to prevent it from being distracted by more global logical considerations. Emotion, of course, plays no part whatever in formal logic. In the SEU theory it is at most linked to the ranking of desires. In Simon's notion of bounded rationality, it helps us to put the problem at hand above the demands of an idealized rationality.

By now it should be evident that thinking of a computer as a logic machine at some level of description is a far cry from being justified in thinking of it as rational, in any humanly recognizable sense of the word. At several points in the discussion, however, I have talked about logic at various "levels of description" in the computer. To appreciate the distinction between the levels of description, and the importance of that distinction, you need to know more about the machines themselves.

---

8.   Ibid., p. 198.

Turing Machines

Now that you know what a formal system is, and a bit about what logic is, it is possible to begin to discuss the machines that automate formal systems.

Imagine a long railroad track, extending indefinitely far in both directions. The railroad ties divide the railroad bed into a series of cells. In some cells there is a single stone; in others there is nothing at all. Now imagine a small flatcar that rides along this track. It has a hole cut in the middle of its floor so that the contents of each cell can be checked. There is also a simple apparatus on it that is capable of (a) determining whether there is or is not a stone in a cell, (b) placing a stone in a cell if there isn't one already there, (c) removing a stone from a cell, (d) moving the cart an arbitrary number of cells in either direction, and (e) following a set of instructions for doing any sequence of (a) through (d).

It turns out that if you are clever enough about writing the instructions, this apparatus is capable of some sophisticated processing. Just as you might do arithmetic by manipulating the beads on an abacus, this machine can do the same by moving about and manipulating stones. Given a sufficiently ingenious set of instructions, the machine could build and inspect some railroad-track analogue of truth-tables; it could test pairs of sentences for logical equivalence and sets of sentences for logical consistency.

Alan Turing analyzed the capabilities and limitations of such machines in considerable detail. In his honor, these machines are called *Turing machines*. When I say "these machines," I am not talking about flatcars and railroad tracks. A Turing machine is any device whose mode of operation is formally equivalent to what I have described above. In addition, any function or process that can be accomplished by a Turing machine with the right set of instructions is said to be *Turing-computable*.

Think of it this way: If a given task can be specified in a finite set of completely unambiguous instructions—also known as an algorithm—then a Turing machine can do it. If a Turing machine can do it, then it is Turing-computable. This claim is called the *Church-Turing thesis*, since it was independently advanced by the mathematician Alonzo Church.

It is important to the idea of a Turing machine that the tokens to be manipulated be unambiguously identifiable, just as it is important to the idea of a formal system. Either there is a stone or there isn't; there must not be any intermediate state. It is also important that the instructions in the algorithm be completely unambiguous, just as in a formal system. There cannot be the sort of instruction that you might find in a cookbook recipe to add "just a bit" of something, or to move to the right "a few times." These instructions are ambiguous; they do not specify a unique operation to be performed. The procedure specified in an unambiguous algorithm is called an *effective method*. If there is an effective method for doing something, then a Turing machine can do it.

An entire branch of mathematics called *decision theory* has emerged as mathematicians (and others) have attempted to understand which processes are Turing-computable and which are not. This sort of thing is particularly interesting when you consider a Turing machine programmed (that is, given a suitable algorithm) to carry out operations within a formal system. One of the most surprising and significant discoveries of this century is the discovery that simple arithmetic, considered as a formal system, is *not* Turing-computable. That is, if you devise a formal system powerful enough to represent arithmetic, that system will contain "formally undecidable" propositions. This was proved by the logician Kurt Gödel and is referred to as "Gödel's Incompleteness Proof."[9]

Digital Computers

A Turing machine, then, is an abstraction, a way of talking about a whole class of devices that are capable of executing algorithms and manipulating tokens according to rules. The logical principles of the Turing machine were thought out by Turing before there were any very sophisticated computers. With those principles in place, it was not long before actual physical devices were built that operated in accordance with them, such as the Colossus machine described in Chapter 1. The device

---

9.   In fact, there were several proofs involving incompleteness.

that has turned out to be the most significant implementation of the Turing-machine concept is the *digital computer*, the structure and operation of which I shall proceed to sketch.

A switch is a device that has two states: on and off. It has no intermediate states and is therefore *digital* in character. Switches that are operated by electric currents are called *relays*. An array of such switches could be used as an efficient replacement for the hypothetical railroad-track device described above. Instead of a flatcar, we would need to be able to get a machine to flip switches on and off according to a set of instructions. The idea is for the system to have a precisely definable set of *discrete states*. As I explained in Chapter 1, the earliest digital computers used banks of vacuum tubes for switches, and the instructions for manipulating them were "hard-wired" into the machine. That is, the machine was designed to execute one algorithm; if you wanted it to do something else you had to go in ·and rewire it for the new task. This is why it was a major breakthrough when the mathematician John Von Neumann conceived of the *stored-program* machine, which could accept and execute different sets of instructions, to manipulate tokens in different ways.

This is an important concept. While an individual Turing machine is able to identify tokens and manipulate them in a particular way, a different Turing machine might work with a different set of instructions and manipulate tokens in an entirely different way. So one machine would operate in a way that we might find convenient to interpret as addition, while the other would operate in a way that we would interpret as subtraction. If you imagine a single machine that is capable of doing what any particular Turing machine can do, that would be a *universal Turing machine* (UTM). A stored-program digital computer is a close approximation of a UTM.[10]

A typical modern digital computer consists of a number of interlocked systems. First, there is an *input device*, which is used to get information or instructions into the machine. In a familiar home computer, the standard input device is a keyboard, but there are others, such as bar-code

---

10. It is only an approximation, of course, since all actual digital computers have limitations of memory (i.e., storage) that abstract Turing machines do not have.

scanners, punch-card readers, and microphones. The purpose of the input device is to accept a physical influence of some sort and to send an appropriate digital code to the machine. In the case of a keyboard, the physical pressure of a finger upon a particular key is sensed and a code is electrically generated. The input device, then, is not completely passive. It not only detects a physical influence of some sort, but also *translates* it into the digital tokens that the computer can manipulate.

Another system is the "main memory" of the computer. In modern computers, this is called "RAM," which is an acronym for *random access memory*. It is called "random access" because any location in the memory can be accessed directly, without having to access the memory locations before or after it. Physically, RAM is contained in an integrated circuit chip that houses thousands or millions of tiny switches embedded in silicon. The integrated circuit chip is the latest replacement for the stones on the railroad bed of the primitive hypothetical Turing machine. Because these switches operate by means of the semiconductor properties of silicon rather than mechanical leverage, they are capable of being manipulated millions of times each second. Keep in mind, then, that the physical tokens manipulated in a modern digital computer are the discrete on and off states of electronic switches embedded in silicon.

Next, there is the *central processing unit*, or CPU. This is the part of the computer that actually executes instructions. The instructions that it is able to execute are rather more sophisticated than what was described for the generic Turing machine, but it nevertheless can only do what such a generic machine could do; it merely does it faster. So the CPU might execute instructions such as "Take the next keyboard input and copy it into registers 1 through 7, then add that to what is already in registers 8 through 15 and put the result in registers 16 through 23." The CPU is constructed in such a way that it can do these addressing, adding, and copying operations extremely quickly.

The computer will also have an *output device* that permits the results of the computations to be physically represented in a way that is useful to humans, such as a video-screen display. Other output devices could be speakers, paper-tape punches, or telephone modems.

Digital computers typically also have *peripheral memory*, usually in the form of magnetic tapes or disks (although optical disks accessed by lasers are now in use). A common use for peripheral memory is to store the programs that the computer executes and to store the results of the processing. The contents of RAM memory, since they consist only of switch settings, are lost when the computer power is turned off, as is the video-screen display. So the peripheral memory serves as a kind of auxiliary input and output device and a long-term memory.

The details will certainly change as more and more sophisticated machines are built. It is possible, for example, that future RAM will use something other than integrated circuits pressed into silicon chips. Whatever the physical principles of operation are, however, the machine of the future will be a digital computer if it has the capability of automating the transformations of a formal system using discrete states as tokens and simulating a Turing machine.

Computers and Other Things

Digital computers are not like other things, even though they may function similarly. Digital and analog clocks differ in more than just the way they display the time. A digital watch contains a small digital computer that is executing a program. The input device is a quartz crystal, whose vibrations are converted to electric pulses. The computer accepts these pulses as input, counts them, and eventually produces output in the form of the numeric display. A mechanical analog clock is powered by spring-driven turning wheels, whose relative sizes and positions move the hands on the clock face. Even though the clock may have ratchets that "digitize" the motion of those wheels by limiting their motion to discrete states, there is no program being executed. The terms "input" and "output" do not seem to work so well. By applying torsion to the clock spring, it could perhaps be said that the clock is accepting input, and the motion of the hands could certainly be considered output.[11] But these are not true input and output

---

11. Indeed, a true digital clock can easily be constructed to push hands around a dial, instead of a numeric display.

because they are never, in the analog clock, coded into the token scheme of a formal system. In the digital clock, the motion of the quartz crystal is used to generate the tokens of a formal system, which are then manipulated according to rules. In the analog clock, the motion of the unwinding spring simply imparts motion to other parts of the clock.

Note that the difference between the digital and analog clocks has nothing to do with the fact that one is electronic and the other is mechanical. A true digital computer could be made out of Tinkertoys powered by a wound spring.[12]

What, precisely, makes a machine a *digital* system? It is the fact that the machine has a finite number of discrete states. That is, there are only so many states that the machine can be in, and it is always in exactly one of those states. Imagine an hourglass in which water is poured from one chamber into the other. Assuming that there is an infinite number of ways to separate the water into two amounts,[13] the water hourglass does not have a finite number of discrete states. Now imagine an hourglass that uses sand. Since there is some finite number of sand particles, there is only a finite number of ways to divide them between the two chambers of the hourglass. At any given moment, the sand hourglass is in a particular digital state.

The sand hourglass may be a digital machine, but it is not a digital computer. Why not? It is because the distribution of grains of sand in the two chambers of the hourglass do not correspond to the permissible configurations of the syntax of a formal system. If it did, then it would be a digital computer.

But now imagine an electronic computer programmed to divide its RAM into two sections. In one section, every memory location has the value 1; in the other section, every memory location has the value 0. The program performs a simple operation: One at a time, it changes the 1's in the first section to 0's and the 0's in the second section to 1's.

---

12.   This has in fact been done by students at MIT.

13.   Yes, this is a false assumption. It is possible to argue that since the material world is ultimately reducible to quanta, *everything* is a digital system, but this argument is merely a distraction here.

When there are no more 1's in the first section, it stops. In short, it is doing with its RAM registers something very much like what the sand hourglass is doing with the individual grains of sand. The single rule of "syntax" is that the total number of 1's must remain constant.

Both "hourglasses" operate according to physical principles. The output of the sand hourglass is determined by the size and mass of the sand particles, gravity, and friction. And that's all. The output of the electronic hourglass is determined by electromagnetic forces, but at a higher level of description its output is determined by *rules*. That is what makes it a digital computer.

This is a very philosophically interesting conclusion. The difference between digital computers and other things is ultimately that digital computers are systems whose behavior is determined by physical laws and rules, whereas other things are simply subject to physical laws. We know (or we think we do) what physical laws are, but what are rules? Is the fact that the sequence of states of a digital computer is rule-governed a physical fact about it? If not, what kind of a fact is it? Can we tell whether something is following rules, and not just physical laws, by taking it apart?

When we talk about a single-purpose computer, like the early machines, with its programming "hard-wired" into it, what are we really saying? We are saying that we have a physical device designed to manipulate physical tokens in one particular way. The electronic hourglass could be such a hard-wired machine. If we are to count the electronic hourglass as a digital computer, then it seems that we must also count the sand hourglass as a digital computer, since it too is a physical device designed to manipulate physical tokens in one particular way.[14]

On the face of it, a stored-program computer is rather different from a hard-wired computer, since the rules that govern its behavior are part of its input. It accepts those rules coded into tokens, and what it does with subsequent tokens of input is determined by those rules. But what

---

14. If you are wondering about whether the *order* of manipulating the tokens matters, imagine a very tall and thin sand hourglass in which the particles are stacked end-to-end before they pass through the aperture.

does this difference really amount to? The tokens—be they "rule-token" strings or "data-token" strings—are physical objects that cause another physical object to behave in a certain way. Token strings are not rules at all until we so interpret them.

This is an interesting turnabout. We said that a digital computer is a machine that can manipulate physical tokens according to the rules of a formal system, without reference to any meaning or interpretation assigned to those tokens. It is a syntax machine. Upon further reflection, however, we discover that *we cannot even say what a rule is, in a way that allows us to distinguish digital computers from other digital systems,*[15] *without assigning meanings to certain tokens and physical states of those systems.*

The point is not that we don't know what digital computers are. We know very well what they are because we have created them to be useful to us in very specific ways. One way to look at it is that a digital computer is readily describable at three levels of description, while things that are not digital computers are readily describable at only two. First, there is the physical level of description. Any physical system at all can be described at this level. Digital computers cannot, however, be distinguished from other things at the physical level of description. There is also the output, or behavioral, level of description. As we saw with the example of the digital and analog clocks, computers cannot be distinguished from other things at this level either.[16] What sets the digital computer apart is that it is readily describable at an intermediate level, at which we can say that it is following certain rules. What we should now also understand is that the fact that the computer is so describable is not a "natural fact" about it; it is a fact about its design and construction, relative to human interests. The manner of operation of a digital computer is readily modified by a computer program, but what makes an object a program? It is the fact that we can assign to it a syntax and a set of

---

15. And, on some interpretations of quantum mechanics, *everything* is a digital system.

16. Another example would be compact-disc versus conventional magnetic-tape audio systems, although audiophiles might dispute this.

transformation rules that conform to the constraints upon formal systems.

The trouble is, if we are clever enough we can assign a syntax and transformation rules to virtually any nonrandom physical process. That is, we can describe any deterministic system *as if* it were a digital computer. The philosopher John Searle (about whom we shall have much more to say in this book) makes the point as follows:

> There is no way you could discover that something is intrinsically a digital computer because the characterization of it as a digital computer is always relative to an observer who assigns a syntactical interpretation to the purely physical features of the system.[17]

Programs and Rules

As has already been mentioned, at the lowest level of description at which it makes sense to describe the digital computer as following rules, the machine is manipulating configurations of switches. The computer's CPU is designed to be able to perform these manipulations according to a small set of rules. Since everything at this level is about the on and off states of switches, it is convenient to represent the computer's rules, input, and output as strings of 1's and 0's. This coding is called *binary machine language*. Ultimately, everything that the computer works with must be coded into this "language."[18]

I hasten to add that it is not really all that convenient for humans to interact with computers by means of this code. We do not easily read, remember, and interpret long strings of 1's and 0's, so the likelihood of error is great. It was therefore not long before *high-level programming*

---

17. John R. Searle, "Is the Brain a Digital Computer?" Presidential Address delivered before the Pacific Division meeting of the American Philosophical Association on March 30, 1990; reprinted in *Proceedings and Addresses of the American Philosophical Association*, 63, no. 3 (November 1990), 28.

18. The quotation marks around the word "language" are a reminder that this sort of coding is only a part of what language is all about. It should be unnecessary to point this out, but there are universities where students are fulfilling "language" requirements by studying computer programming languages.

languages were developed. These languages are themselves programs written in a low-level language whose function is to make it easier for humans to compose and modify algorithms for the computer to execute. The high-level programming languages allow the programmer to use terms such as "if" and "while" and the familiar mathematical operators in familiar, though rigidly defined, ways. These languages also allow the programmer to assign convenient names to objects that the computer is to manipulate, without having to think about their digital memory addresses. For example, look at the following tiny program fragment, written in the high-level language Pascal:

```
program average;
begin
     read(alice,bill,carol);
     student_number:=3;
     total_score:=alice+bill+carol;
     average:=total_score/student_number;
     if average > 60 then
     print("Passing")
     else print("Failing");
end.
```

The first line simply announces the name of the program. The second line indicates that the sequence of instructions begins at the next line. The third line says that the computer is going to associate token strings with the three names "alice," "bill," and "carol." What strings is it going to associate with them? It will use the strings that it "reads" from some input device, perhaps a keyboard. The fourth line uses the operator ":=" to instruct the computer to associate the number 3 with the name "student_number." This is sometimes called an "assignment statement," because it assigns a value to a name, or "identifier." The fifth line assigns to yet another identifier the sum of the values associated with "alice," "bill," and "carol." The sixth line assigns to an identifier called "average" the result of dividing "total_score" by "student_number." The seventh line is a *conditional instruction*. What the computer does depends upon the value associated with the identifier "average." The last line tells the computer that there are no more instructions.

This program is very simple, but it illustrates what it is to get a computer to follow rules. You can't just "tell" the computer to average the scores (unless your computer has a built-in function to do just that). You must give the computer exact instructions in terms of the basic things that it *does* know how to do, represented in the unambiguous syntax of the programming language. The computer can only follow the rules that a programmer can represent in this sort of a code. If you were programming a computer to play chess, you might want to instruct the machine to "try to capture pieces until the opponent puts his king into an exposed position." That may make perfect sense to you as a rule, but for the computer to use it you will have to find a way to state it in a formal programming language.

Keep in mind, then, that a central claim of artificial intelligence is that all intelligent activities can be "captured" by sets of rules in some programming language.

Chapter 4

The Turing Test

In Chapter 1, I referred to a short paper by Alan Turing that appeared in 1950 in the philosophy journal *Mind*; its title was "Computing Machinery and Intelligence."[1] It would not be an exaggeration to say that this paper permanently transformed the way people think about the mind-body problem. In fact, there are many who believe that Turing solved the problem in one stroke. This seems to be particularly true of computer scientists working in the field of AI, many of whom seem to think that Turing wrote in his paper everything they will ever need to know about this philosophical issue. So Turing's position has come to have a foundational status in the AI field.

This means no more, however, than that these scientists would like to get on with the nonfoundational work without troubling about vexing philosophical arguments and counterarguments. It is a common enough posture for scientists to adopt toward the foundational aspects of their disciplines. It does not mean that we should accept that the mind-body problem is "solved."

What, then, did Turing write that had such a galvanizing effect? I will summarize the key points here, but the original article is not especially technical and should be read by anyone who is interested in this subject.

---

1. *Mind* 59 (1950); reprinted in *Minds and Machines*, ed. Alan Ross Anderson, pp. 4–30.

The Turing Test Itself

First, Turing described something that he called the "Imitation Game." In the Imitation Game there are three players in separate rooms who communicate by teletype machines. (We may prefer to think in terms of more modern equipment, such as computer-terminal screens.) Let's call them "Player A," "Player B," and "Player C." Players A and B are not of the same sex; Player C can be a man or a woman. The object of the game is for Player C to try to guess who is a woman and who is a man pretending to be a woman. The only information that Player C can have about Players A and B, however, is what he can get by typing questions or comments to them and reading their responses. If a player is in fact a woman, she should just reply in a natural manner to what Player C writes. If he is a man, he should attempt to answer the questions in a way that will convince Player C that he is a woman.

Having thus described the Imitation Game, Turing went on to describe a variation on it. He wrote:

> We now ask the question, "What will happen when a machine takes the part of A in this game?" Will the interrogator decide wrongly as often when the game is played like this as he does when the game is played between a man and a woman? These questions replace our original "Can machines think?"[2]

In the extensive literature on this article, a number of simplified variations of the latter version of the game have been proposed. One common variation has only two players, A and B. Player A's task is to guess whether B is a human or a computer pretending to be one. This variation of the Imitation Game is what has come to be called the "Turing Test." It's worth taking note of the fact, however, that there is a significant difference between Turing's own version and the variation that has taken its place in the literature. As Turing describes it, the interrogator is still trying to guess the gender of his interlocutors; he is not trying to expose a mechanical impostor and is apparently unaware of this dimension of the game. In the newer version, the interlocutor knows that

---

2.   Ibid., p. 5.

Player B is either a human or a machine, and that that is precisely what is at issue. Gender is irrelevant, except insofar as it might be a source of clues for detecting humanity or its absence.

Presumably, the newer version of the game—which I shall henceforth refer to simply as the Turing Test—is more demanding of the computer, since Player A's line of questioning is likely to be more focused on the relevant issue: Is Player B a human or a computer? In fact, Turing's own version is confusing. He asks if the human interrogator will "decide wrongly" as often as he would if A and B were both humans. But what counts as deciding wrongly here? If a single guess consists of attributing a gender to both A and B, then C will "decide wrongly" every time, since A is neither a man nor a woman. Player C has not been asked to comment on whether he is confident that both A and B are human beings. In essence, Turing's version of the game asks C to notice whether the game is being played according to the rules at all.

Fortunately, in his subsequent commentary, Turing himself begins to treat the game as if it were a game in which a human tries to decide whether she is interacting with another human or a machine. It is interesting, however, that the transition to what is now called the Turing Test was not explicitly noted by Turing himself.

We need to consider what would count as winning this game, or passing the Turing Test. To do so, imagine a few additional conditions. Suppose, for example, that there is a time limit of, say, a half-hour for the test. In addition, suppose that a single "test" actually includes a whole series of such half-hour interviews, with different questioners. Given these conditions, we may say that a computer "passes" the Turing Test if it performs as well as an actual human being. That is, if it is as likely that human questioners will take the programmed computer to be a human as it is that they will take a randomly selected human to be a human, we may say that *in general* human questioners cannot distinguish it from a human.

As simple as even this sounds, a moment's reflection shows that there are some slippery aspects to the Turing Test. For one thing, Player A's—the interrogator's—strategy and decision will be strongly influenced by her general beliefs about the capabilities of computers. To see this, think about how difficult or easy it might be for a human being to *fail* the Turing Test. Some humans are not very good at expressing themselves verbally (especially in writing). If Player A thinks that there are, or might be, computers that are very close to being able to perform at a human level on this test, then she might be more likely to be duped by a somewhat inept human. If, on the other hand, she is quite sure that no computer can even come close to this level of performance, then she will probably be more tolerant of B's errors. Furthermore, somebody who has given a lot of thought to artificial intelligence is likely to have many more ideas about the sorts of errors a programmed computer, as opposed to a human, would be prone to. The most demanding version of the Turing Test, then, would have a *sophisticated* human (in matters concerning AI) doing the interrogating.

The "Strong AI" Thesis

Turing's point was simple: If a computer can pass the Turing Test (although Turing himself, of course, did not call it that), then we know all that we need to know in order to decide that it is intelligent.

Although Turing himself limited his remarks to the property called "intelligence" and the question of whether machines can "think," others have been eager to generalize his conclusions to cover any and all mental states and properties. According to this extended thesis, the Turing Test–passing computer may be said to be not just intelligent but conscious, with a mental life, ideas, beliefs, desires, and whatever else goes with having a mind. Put another way, the thesis is that the ability to pass the Turing Test is a logically sufficient condition for having a mind.

Often, when first considering this thesis, people begin to complain that no computer could ever perform indistinguishably from a human on this or that aspect of the Turing Test. They may assert, for example, that no programmed computer could possibly "get" jokes, or puns, or metaphors, or whatever. While there is a point to entertaining such objections—and we shall do so later—it is important to understand that they do not address the central philosophical point. These objections pertain to the question of whether we shall ever have programmed computers that can pass the Turing Test. This is undoubtedly an interesting and important question, since it calls upon us to consider just what kinds of capabilities a machine would have to have in order to succeed, but it is still a side-issue. Let's assume, for the sake of the argument, that eventually some programmed computer *will* pass the Turing Test. The real philosophical issue that is at stake is whether we want to go along with Turing and conclude that the fact that some computer passes the Turing Test is a sufficient condition for its having a mind.

The philosopher John Searle is one of the key players in the dispute surrounding Turing's claim, and we shall soon consider his arguments in detail. He has called Turing's claim the "strong AI thesis," the claim that "the appropriately programmed computer really *is* a mind, in the sense that computers given the right programs can be literally said to *understand* and have other cognitive states."[3] What is the "right program"? How do we decide if a computer is "appropriately" programmed? Oddly, Searle makes no explicit comment on this in his original paper. In a later essay in *Scientific American*, however, he characterizes the approach of the strong AI community as follows:

> [T]hey believe that by designing the right programs with the right inputs and outputs, they are literally creating minds. They believe furthermore that they have a scientific test for determining success or failure: the Turing Test devised by Alan M. Turing, the founding father of artificial intelligence.[4]

Clearly, what Searle means by the "right program" is the program that will enable the computer to pass the Turing Test. It is an open question whether strong AI really does represent a commitment of most or many researchers in AI. Many may, in the end, be committed only to "weak AI," which is simply the view that the study of the mind can be advanced by developing and studying computer models of various men-

---

3. John Searle, "Minds, Brains, and Programs," *Behavioral and Brain Sciences*, 3 (1980); reprinted in *The Mind's I*, ed. Douglas R. Hofstadter and Daniel C. Dennett (New York: Bantam Books, 1981), p. 353.

4. John Searle, "Is the Brain's Mind a Computer Program?" *Scientific American*, 262, no. 1 (January 1990), 26.

tal processes. Although weak AI is of considerable methodological interest in cognitive science, it is not of much philosophical interest. Strong
AI, on the other hand, incorporates a substantive philosophical doctrine.
Because Searle's work has been so widely discussed, the "strong AI" label
has gained wide usage.

The first thing to do is to consider why the strong AI thesis has any
plausibility at all.

The Case for Strong AI

First, there is the matter of simplicity. The Turing Test is not complicated
and the strong AI thesis does not depend upon any obscure metaphysical
principles. At least, it doesn't at first glance seem to depend upon any
such principles. By comparison, Cartesian dualism is much more complex, requiring the division of the world into two very different categories
of being that nevertheless manage to interact causally. Simplicity is a
strong point in favor of strong AI among scientists, who may be somewhat
prone to distrust elaborate philosophical systems. This attitude is based
on the scientists' recognition that in the past these philosophical systems
seemed to block the advance of science. Cartesian dualism itself held that
nothing is more evident and accessible to the mind than itself. Therefore,
the notion of a "subconscious mind," as put forward by Freud and others,
seemed to be a contradiction in terms. Dualism was an obstacle to the
very possibility of a serious scientific investigation into the matter.

More important even than its simplicity is the fact that the strong AI
thesis proposes a partially objective method for determining the presence of intelligence. Even though the interrogators make subjective
judgments about the systems with which they are interacting, the
system for dealing with these judgments in the aggregate is quite
objective. There is no vagueness in the rules of the test and no difficulty
in interpreting the outcome. The results of the procedure are publicly
observable. Scientific progress in many fields has depended upon the
development of such objective and public methods, so it seems appropriate to prefer them in considering questions of artificial intelligence, too.

In fact, the strong AI thesis proposes an *operational* definition of the mind: A mind is whatever set of functional capabilities will enable a system to behave in ways characteristic of systems already known to have minds, and those capabilities are detected by the Turing Test. This definition gains its power precisely by sidestepping any questions as to *how* the system achieves these capabilities. Mind is a logical function of what a system can do, regardless of how it does it, on this account. For this reason, the strong AI thesis is sometimes said to offer a "black box" theory of the mind.

"Black box" is an old engineering term used to refer to a part of a device that does some specifiable job, even though the engineer hasn't yet figured out just how she will get that part to work. In our context, the term "black box" means that we don't care about the details of the process that enables the system to pass the Turing Test. We don't care about its material composition either. Whether it is made of wet gray matter or tiny integrated circuits, it is all the same to this theory. All we care about is that it can pass for a human, under certain clearly definable and publicly observable conditions. If there are two machines that both pass the Turing Test, we don't care if they are structurally or materially similar or dissimilar; they are both intelligent systems to which all mental terms truly apply.

Another aspect of the strong AI thesis that appears to count in its favor is the apparent *impartiality* of the Turing Test. If Player B were an extraterrestrial instead of a computer or a human being, its possibly exotic appearance, physical composition, or biological structure would not count against it in our attempt to determine whether it has a mind. There are strong intuitive reasons for thinking that such factors *shouldn't* count. It would be "human chauvinism" to insist that all intelligent beings must resemble us in some physically specifiable ways. Even to insist that intelligent beings must be *alive* is apparently an instance of "biochauvinism." Contemporary biological science has opted for a functional definition of "alive" anyway; life is whatever performs all or most "life functions," such as assimilation, excretion, and reproduction. But what do these processes have to do with intelligence, mind, and consciousness? It seems entirely arbitrary to hold to these life functions as necessary conditions for something that is quite different from them:

mind. The fact that minds have so far only been associated with living things ought not to blind us to the possibility, at least, that they could be associated with nonliving things, or things whose status as living or nonliving cannot be decided.

The strong AI thesis purports to use the Turing Test to filter out what is irrelevant to mind and to isolate what is essential to it. In Turing's own words, "The new problem [i.e., the Turing Test] has the advantage of drawing a fairly sharp line between the physical and the intellectual capacities of a man."[5] So the plausibility of the strong AI thesis depends upon the extent to which it does indeed capture what is essential to intelligence.

In the Turing Test, the participants exchange typed texts via some simple electronic apparatus. The fact that they are typed—on paper or on-screen—is simply a condition that eliminates the possibility of handwriting cues. The fact that they are *texts* is all-important. What the Turing Test in fact tests is the ability to generate "appropriate" output texts in response to input texts. If we were speaking strictly of humans, we would say that the ability to generate the appropriate texts demonstrates *understanding* of the input texts. We refer to these abilities together as "literacy." In philosophy, it is often referred to as "linguistic competence." Now, "understanding" is clearly a mental term; it refers to one of the things that we routinely accomplish by means of intelligence. If the ability to generate appropriate output really does demonstrate understanding, then the strong AI thesis must be correct.

Turing was not the first to single out linguistic competence as intimately associated with mind. Over three hundred years ago, Descartes claimed that the one thing that no automaton would never be able to do is use and understand language. The ability to use language seems to indicate intelligence in a way that nothing else does. This is the central intuition behind the strong AI thesis. In the next chapter, we shall examine this intuition in more detail. It is a strong intuition, however. Speaking and understanding in one's native language do not feel very mechanical. When one is just learning a new language, using it may feel

---

5.   Turing, "Computing Machinery and Intelligence," p. 5.

mechanical and rule-bound for a while, but mastery of that language consists precisely of shedding that feeling.

Another thing to note about the strong AI thesis is that it is *behavioral*. This means that a system's mental capacities are defined (or at least identified) by its behavior. As I have already explained, behaviorism has had a powerful influence upon contemporary philosophy, due to its insistence that the only proper subject matter for scientific psychology is behavior, because only behavior is publicly observable and measurable. I have reviewed some of the difficulties of behaviorism, but that should not be taken to mean that strong AI was doomed from the start. The strong AI thesis is a variant of behaviorism that takes into account many of those difficulties. It is different in a number of respects from its parent doctrines. The difference lies in the restricted range of behavior that the strong AI thesis recognizes as relevant to the mind: textual output. Behaviorism in general, philosophical or psychological, makes no such restriction. Using the computer scientist's shorthand "I/O" to stand for "input/output," an accurate name for the philosophy of mind based upon the strong AI thesis would be "textual I/O behaviorism." This name, however, does not appear in the literature. Instead, the label "Turing machine functionalism" is used. Searle himself remarks that,

> [I]n much of AI there is a residual behaviorism or operationalism. Since appropriately programmed computers can have input-output patterns similar to those of human beings, we are tempted to postulate mental states in the computer similar to human mental states.[6]

Finally, in considering the case for the strong AI thesis, it is necessary to consider what sort of thesis it is. It is not a thesis about the capabilities or limitations of any contemporary or future computing machines. It is not the claim that the mind is a computer, nor that the brain is a computer, whatever such claims might mean. It is instead a thesis about the logically sufficient conditions for attributing intelligence and other mental properties to something. So it is a *logical* thesis, not a *technological* one. This will have to be kept in mind as we think about criticisms.

---

6.   Searle, "Minds, Brains, and Programs," p. 371.

The Jukebox Argument

What is the proper way to go about criticizing something like the strong AI thesis? Some may find it counterintuitive without being able to say just why. One way to proceed is to search for counterexamples. In this case, a counterexample would be a case of something that could pass the Turing Test, but which anyone (especially a defender of the strong AI thesis) would agree lacks mental properties. What this really amounts to is testing the thesis against the set of concepts that we already have in place. These concepts structure our intuitions about things, so if we can find a counterexample we have likely found that the strong AI thesis is inconsistent with something that we already believe. The next thing to do is to isolate precisely the intuition that is the source of the conflict and weigh it against the new thesis and the arguments that go with it.

You might not immediately trust this appeal to "intuitions" at the heart of an allegedly objective investigation. Perhaps this method of doing things can be clarified by means of an interesting and widely accepted model of beliefs and belief change. The philosopher W. V. O. Quine has characterized the system of beliefs of any person as a kind of web, with each belief depending upon others. The critical process that I have been describing may be thought of as the attempt to add to, or modify, a bit of the web of belief. The search for counterexamples is a kind of "damage check." If we find that the strong AI thesis logically forces us to discard some other beliefs that are very well secured in the web, then we have good reason to be suspicious of it. Much philosophical activity consists of such conceptual damage control.

The first counterexample that I want to present was devised by the philosopher Ned Block of MIT.[7] First, recall a detail of the Turing Test:

---

7. In fact, I modify the scenario somewhat, but the principle is the same. Block himself did not characterize his imaginary machine as a jukebox, but the comparison has seemed apt to many who have discussed it, and the name has stuck. The argument was presented in his "Troubles with Functionalism," in *Perception and Cognition: Issues in the Foundations of Psychology,* ed. C.W. Savage, Minnesota Studies in the Philosophy of Science, vol. 9 (Minneapolis: University of Minnesota Press, 1978), pp. 261–325; reprinted in *Readings in Philosophy of Psychology,* ed. Ned Block, vol. 1, (Cambridge, Mass.: Harvard University Press, 1980), pp. 268-305.

It is timed. Consider that there are only a finite number of sentences that can be exchanged by the Turing Test players in a half-hour. That number is unthinkably large, to be sure, but it is finite. Imagine that each possible sentence, then, is stored on a little tape in the memory of a giant jukebox. Also in its memory is a set of instructions of the form, "If the input sentence is number 548,383,100,355, then output sentence number 1,336,396,448." This set of instructions must also be very large. And that is the *only* kind of capability it has. It accepts an input sentence, looks it up in a long list, and plays back an output sentence. It acts, in effect, like a giant jukebox of "canned" sentences.

This machine would really be impossibly large; it is a pure thought experiment and should not for a moment be taken to be a practical approach to the problem. But thought experiments have their uses. We need to consider whether this sort of jukebox machine could, in principle, pass the Turing Test. One objection might be that there is more to passing the Turing Test than simply responding appropriately to the last sentence. In a real conversation, earlier sentences matter too. We often refer to things said much earlier; a machine that couldn't do so would be easily exposed. This is a reasonable objection, but the imaginary sentence-playing jukebox can be fixed to meet it. We will still have the same library of canned sentences, but we will alter the rules a bit. They will be of the form, "If the sequence of sentences so far has been 100,245, followed by 506, followed by 1,245,747,699,012 . . . and so on, then output sentence 3." There should be a rule of that sort for every possible sequence of sentences producible in a half-hour Turing Test.

This modification increases the necessary size of the jukebox by many orders of magnitude, but that doesn't matter. In our thought experiment, we are allowing ourselves as many universes as we need to build it. It should be clear that this sort of machine could and would pass the Turing Test because, in essence, every possible Turing Test conversation has been foreseen by its builders and the replies have been built in. The point, however, is that there is nothing in the least intelligent about this machine. It works on exactly the same principles as the jukebox in your local pizza parlor, a machine to which no one would be inclined to attribute intelligence. It's just a lot bigger.

It is important to consider just what it is that is missing in this Olympian jukebox in virtue of which we deny that it is intelligent. An obvious point is that this machine does not *analyze* the sentences presented to it, nor does it *compose* the output sentences. Instead, it simply *matches* the input to an entry in a list, retrieves the output sentence, and plays it back. It doesn't process anything subsentential in scale. When people use and understand language, on the other hand, they process utterances in a way that involves identifying the components of sentences and generating new sentences from subsentential elements (such as words). This sort of processing is an important part of what we mean by "understanding." The giant jukebox may be very good at playing back the right sentences, but it doesn't understand anything.

If it is logically possible that there could be a machine that could pass the Turing Test without understanding anything, then simply passing the Turing Test cannot be a logically sufficient condition for understanding, which is an important part of intelligence. The strong AI thesis is therefore undermined by this counterexample. That is, Ned Block believes that if we must choose between the strong AI thesis and the denial of intelligence to the jukebox—and the thought experiment is designed to force precisely that choice upon us—then we must choose the latter. The attribution of intelligence to the jukebox is an unacceptably high intuitive price to pay for the strong AI thesis.

Some have complained that the jukebox scenario is simply too fantastic to mean anything. This machine would vastly overflow the bounds of the known universe; what good is a conclusion based upon such preposterous premises? I think one could reply that it is no more preposterous than Einstein's thought experiments in which he asked us to imagine riding on the end of a beam of light and consider what the universe would look like from there. The *logical* point remains the same. Still, it is worth digressing to describe an actual computer program that operates in a manner not unlike that of our hypothetical jukebox.

The program, which was first mentioned in Chapter 1, is called ELIZA, and it is quite famous in AI circles. It was written in the

1960s by Joseph Weizenbaum, a computer scientist at MIT. (We shall meet Weizenbaum again in a later chapter.) ELIZA was created as an experiment in "natural language processing," which is simply the attempt to get computers to deal with natural languages, like English, instead of special computer languages. Weizenbaum's idea was to write a program that would mimic the responses of a nondirective therapist, the sort of psychotherapist who does not say much but simply echoes back what the patient has said. A session with a nondirective therapist might look like this (therapist's remarks are in capital letters):

> "I feel depressed."
> "TELL ME WHY YOU FEEL DEPRESSED."
> "I think I can't succeed at anything."
> "YOU THINK YOU CAN'T SUCCEED AT ANYTHING."
> "Yes, that's right."
> "PLEASE TELL ME MORE ABOUT WHY YOU FEEL
> DEPRESSED."

And so on. Weizenbaum was able to write a program that was quite good at this sort of interaction. Versions of his program are now widely available on microcomputers. It is not a very large program. It takes the input sentence, searches it for cue words, tries to change verbs from first person to second person, and perhaps adds a tag such as "Please tell me more about. . . ." If it can't "parse" the input sentence, nor find an interesting cue word, it will play back one of its canned sentences, such as "What else do you want to tell me about this?"

ELIZA was a great success in that it does a creditable job of imitating the nondirective therapist. To Weizenbaum's dismay, some people actually began to take the program seriously as a surrogate therapist. We shall return in a later chapter to the implications of that enthusiasm, but for now we may simply note that ELIZA in fact passes a restricted form of the Turing Test, as long as the human participant "plays along." That is, it is quite easy to expose ELIZA's limitations if you begin to engage in even very simple wordplay or unusual sentence structure. Still, the program is astonishingly good at faking understanding, if you consider that it consists mainly of a modify-and-playback subroutine and a modest library of canned sentences. But nobody supposes for a moment that ELIZA is an intelligent program. And again, we base that judgment not so much on what ELIZA does or fails to do as on our knowledge of how ELIZA works. That shows that our judgment of ELIZA's intelligence is intuitively informed by our knowledge of what is going on in the "black box." The strong AI thesis, however, says that we ought not to *care* what goes on in there. The jukebox/ELIZA counterexample challenges just that stipulation.

It may be argued that the literate jukebox does exhibit a great deal of intelligence, but that that intelligence is embodied in a way that is different from what we are used to. On this line of reasoning, while the simple "look-up" routines involved may be entirely unsophisticated, the intelligence of the system is built into the enormous lists of conditional instructions, which cover every Turing Test contingency. Unlike the simple pizza-parlor jukebox, this set of instructions is vast and intricate.

It is certainly true that there is much intelligence embodied in the literate jukebox. But I would argue that it is not the right sort of embodiment, from the standpoint of AI. By analogy, there is a great deal of intelligence embodied in a set of encyclopedias, but nobody supposes that the volumes themselves are therefore intelligent (or possess any other mental attributes). The intelligence embodied in the jukebox is of this sort. It is static, an *achievement* of intelligence, but it is not itself intelligent. It doesn't *do* anything intelligent; it merely acts mechanically upon some very intelligently arranged and linked lists.

To sum up, Ned Block's argument works by forcing us to make an intuitive link between an intelligent *performance* and the mechanism by which that performance is produced. The next criticism of the strong AI thesis that we shall consider also forces us to look beneath the surface of Turing Test–passing behavior but is different from Block's in that it makes use of our intuitive understanding of understanding.

John Searle's Chinese Room Argument

John Searle coined the term "strong AI thesis" in a paper entitled "Minds, Brains, and Programs," which appeared in an interdisciplinary journal called *Behavioral and Brain Sciences*.[8] In this hotly disputed paper, Searle devises a thought experiment that, like Block's, is both ingenious and somewhat fantastic. As we shall see, however, Searle's argument has some additional and far-reaching implications. They are so far-reaching, indeed, that this argument has become the focal point of dispute in the philosophy of AI.

The thought experiment itself is fairly simple to present. Imagine that you are locked in a small room, seated at a desk. On the right wall is a slot through which sheets of paper are occasionally slipped to you. On these sheets of paper are various marks, straight and curved lines arranged in complex patterns. To you, these patterns are quite meaningless. On the table in front of you is a large and complex manual, written in English. As pages with markings are fed in through the slot, you look through the manual for instructions. The instructions tell you to take a fresh sheet of paper and write marks on it, somewhat similar to the ones on the sheet that was passed to you. The precise configuration of marks that you are instructed to make depends upon what marks were on the sheets that have already come in through the slot.

It's a long and tedious process, looking up instructions in this gigantic manual, but eventually you finish and pass the new page out through a slot in the left-hand wall. Once again, none of these marks mean anything to you. You do not know that the marks on the page being passed to you are in fact questions, written in Chinese, since you are totally unfamiliar with the Chinese language. You also do not know that the marks that the manual instructs you to write on the new sheet of paper are answers to those questions. In fact, they are perfectly *appropriate* answers, so much so that they constitute passing the Turing Test

---

8. John Searle, "Minds, Brains, and Programs," *Behavioral and Brain Sciences*, 3 (1980), pp. 417-24; the paper is already a classic and has been reprinted in several other books.

in Chinese. For you, however, it's just so much busywork. You do not understand any of it except the instructions in the manual.

In this thought experiment, you are part of a system that passes the Turing Test and therefore, according to the strong AI thesis, understands Chinese. Furthermore, in this scenario the manual of instructions represents the alleged computer program that would enable a computer to pass the Turing Test. You are simply acting as the CPU, the central processing unit, of the computer. Any computer program, after all, could be translated into a set of English instructions for a human to follow. But keep in mind that these instructions are not a dictionary of any sort. There is nothing in the manual that says "This symbol means 'banana'." There are only instructions for locating and writing marks on paper. The central idea is that you are put in this room to do exactly what a computer would do if programmed to pass the Turing Test; you are executing a formal program. According to Searle, it doesn't matter if the program is a relatively simple one, such as ELIZA, or more sophisticated, such as the program BORIS mentioned in Chapter 1. Since you can apparently execute this program without understanding any Chinese, it must be a mistake to suppose that executing such a program is sufficient to produce understanding.

Let's review the logic of the argument. According to the strong AI thesis, *anything* that passes the Turing Test can be truly said to have mental states and properties, of which understanding is one. That claim entails that if a programmed computer can pass the Turing Test, then it genuinely understands what is being "said" to it and what its responses mean.[9] Searle is arguing that, if this is the case, then anything that does just what the computer does ought to understand its input and output. But a human being placed in just this position would understand nothing, so the strong AI thesis must be false.

Searle's argument gets its force from the fact that we are all directly aware of what it is to understand language, even though we may not be able to say just what that understanding amounts to. So he does not have

---

9. The strong AI thesis does not claim, of course, that *only* programmed computers can pass the Turing Test, but its proponents are obviously interested mainly in such machines.

to appeal to a theory of understanding so much as to our intuitive understanding of understanding. We could do just what the computer does and still understand nothing, so there is no reason to suppose that the computer understands anything either, Turing Test results notwithstanding.

It is important to appreciate the difference between the Chinese Room argument and the jukebox argument. Although they both employ the logical strategy of offering counterexamples to the strong AI thesis, they are quite different in their consequences. In the jukebox argument, Block appeals to our intuitive sense that jukeboxes, no matter how large, are machines devoid of mental properties. But the argument says nothing at all about whether some other kind of Turing Test–passing machine, such as a digital computer, might be a better candidate for mental attributes. In short, the jukebox argument simply points out the logical inadequacy of the Turing Test as a sufficient condition of any mental states.

The Chinese Room argument reaches deeper. There are no canned sentences here. We shall grant that the manual provides instructions for performing a full syntactic analysis of the input sentences, breaking them down into clauses and words. And we further grant that it puts the output sentences together by means of some complex generative grammatical theory. So we are granting that these instructions allow the person in the room (or a machine programmed according to these instructions) to do some of the very kinds of things that a jukebox doesn't do. We can even grant that the "appropriately programmed" computer performs the same formal operations as the human brain (if it should turn out to be correct to describe brain processes in this way). Even granting all this, Searle argues, the system does not understand Chinese. To do that, it must be able to do more than formal operations on syntactically defined tokens.

The basic nature of digital computers as token-manipulators was explained in an earlier chapter. There, it was pointed out that what digital computers do is manipulate discrete tokens in configurations that are (or can be made to be) meaningful to people and according to rules that allow those configurations to occur in useful sequences. For the moment, let's imagine that it is really a computer in the little room, instead of a person with a manual. The computer is able to scan the input characters and translate them into its own internal system of tokens, according to some code. Its program—the "manual"—then puts it through a long and complex series of configurations at blinding speed, and at some point composes a reply, as opposed to simply playing one back.

Searle's point is that while this sort of thing may well be called "natural language processing" and may very well enable some computer to pass the Turing Test, it is not sufficient for understanding. More generally, no system has mental states *solely* in virtue of its capabilities as a token-manipulator, according to Searle, no matter how sophisticated the processing may be. Understanding depends upon something else entirely. The something else that understanding depends upon is, according to Searle, the "causal powers" of the system. What this might mean is a complex topic to which we shall return in a later chapter. For now, it is sufficient to note that Searle is arguing that even if it turns out to be appropriate to describe the brain as performing formal operations in the information-processing sense, it must also be doing *more* than that. That other part of what the brain does, he claims, is inextricably involved in its ability to produce understanding and other intentional states.

Searle is not, by the way, claiming that artificial intelligence is impossible. He is claiming that nothing, be it a computer or a brain, has mental states solely in virtue of its properties as a token-manipulator or information processor. Like Block, he is insisting that it really does matter what is happening in the "black box," but not in the sense in which some strong AI people might agree with him: They might insist that the "right" sort of program be executed in there. Searle is making the point that if what is happening in there is simply the automated manipulation of tokens—no matter what the algorithm—then there is no possibility that understanding or any other mental event is occurring. It is nevertheless possible in principle on Searle's view for a man-made machine to have the right "causal powers," and therefore to enjoy mental states. I mention this because Searle has occasionally been read as claiming that only biological systems—living things—can have mental states, but this is not what he is claiming. He writes,

> For any artefact that we might build which had mental states equivalent to human mental states, the implementation of a computer program would not by itself be sufficient. Rather the artefact would have to have powers equivalent to the powers of the human brain.[10]

He is not, therefore, a biochauvinist or vitalist, despite the complaints of some of his critics.

This brief survey by no means exhausts the literature of arguments that have been proposed to discredit the Turing Test and the strong AI thesis. I have chosen these two because they are especially clear and vivid and strike at the heart of the matter. Needless to say, the community of Turing Test enthusiasts has not given up in the face of these arguments. Before bringing this chapter to a conclusion, it will be useful to consider some replies to the arguments.

Some Replies to Block and Searle

One thing that Block's and Searle's arguments have in common is that they are both fantastic. There really is not room in the known universe for the machine that Block describes, and it would take years for the person in Searle's Chinese room (given the likely complexity of a Turing Test-passing program) to compute a single response. We need to consider whether these facts are relevant to the philosophical claims that these scenarios underwrite. Or is it possible that some relevant facts are being masked by these fantastic scenarios?

One of the more eloquent writers on these subjects, and an ardent supporter of the Turing Test, is Douglas R. Hofstadter. In an imaginative dialogue written for *Scientific American*, he has one of his characters say,

> Anybody who thinks that somehow a program could be rigged up just to pull sentences out of storage like records in a jukebox, and that this program could pass the Turing Test, has not thought very hard about it. The funny part about it is that it is just this kind of unrealizable

---

10. John Searle, *Minds, Brains and Science* (Cambridge, Mass.: Harvard University Press, 1984), p. 41.

program that some enemies of artificial intelligence cite when arguing against the concept of the Turing Test.[11]

The reference to Block's argument is clear, even though it would be irresponsible to characterize Block as an "enemy of artificial intelligence." Hofstadter apparently feels that Block is guilty of a kind of misdirection in this argument. By getting us to think of his machine as "just" a sentence-retrieval apparatus, he gets us to overlook the complexity and sophistication of the retrieval. We are inclined, according to Hofstadter, to underestimate the intelligence of such a device.

Hofstadter is quite right about this, if we consider a jukebox that has to make a *decision* about which canned sentence to play back, based upon its analysis of the input sentence. Recall, however, that we amended the thought experiment somewhat to disallow this. Instead of matching single input sentences to single output sentences, the second version of jukebox matches *lists* of sentences—of which the current input sentence is simply the last—against internally stored lists, and then looks up and plays back the output sentence. So all of the machine's internal rules are of the form "Add input sentence to list, find resultant list in memory, and play back linked sentence." It's just (1) update list, (2) find list in memory, and (3) output sentence. Since there is nothing particularly sophisticated about this mode of operation, it follows that the sheer scale of the imaginary machine does not mask a genuinely intelligent manner of operation.

Furthermore, Hofstadter's very reply betrays a turning away from the strong AI thesis. Remember, it is a "black box" theory, and we are not supposed to care about what enables the device to pass the Turing Test. By suggesting that Block has misdirected us in the thought experiment to overlook the (allegedly) necessarily intelligent manner of operation of the jukebox, Hofstadter is in fact basing his reply to Block upon a sneak peek into the black box. He is in effect saying, "But look,

---

11.   Douglas R. Hofstadter, "Metamagical Themas: A Coffeehouse Conversation on the Turing Test to Determine if a Machine Can Think," *Scientific American* (May 1981), pp. 15-36.

there really must be intelligent things going on in there." In defending the Turing Test against a critic, Hofstadter reveals that something other than Turing Test–passing is at the heart of his own understanding of intelligence.

There is another "misdirection" argument that Searle himself considers in his original paper. If we take seriously the idea that the instruction manual in the little room contains the equivalent of a computer program for passing the Turing Test in Chinese, then we must recognize that the person in there is only *part* of the overall system, and not necessarily the most important part. It is arguable that the Chinese-understanding of the system resides in the manual itself and that if we consider the system as a whole—and not just the person in the room—it *is* appropriate to attribute understanding to it.

Searle in fact considers this reply in his article; he dubs it the "Systems Reply." To answer it, he suggests an amendment of the conditions of the thought experiment. This time, let the person in the room have the entire instruction manual *memorized,* so that none of the "natural language processing" takes place outside of that person's own mind. Even under these circumstances, the person would still only be manipulating meaningless marks according to complex memorized rules; she still would not understand anything in virtue of following those rules.

As I mentioned at the beginning of this section, the instruction manual for passing the Turing Test (in any language) would be incredibly large and complex. Producing a single output sentence might involve carrying out millions or billions of instructions. The idea of memorizing this manual is indeed fantastic—fantastic in terms of scale, but it is not clear that this is philosophically objectionable.

The literature of comments for and against Searle's Chinese Room argument is extensive. Some of them will serve as focal points of subsequent chapters of this book. Before moving on to those chapters, however, I want to consider one argument in more detail. It anticipates some problems that will be addressed in later chapters. Working through this argument here will help to provide a context for those problems later.

The Robot Reply

I have already pointed out that the strong AI thesis could be dubbed "textual I/O behaviorism." We have also taken note of the fact that the isolation of a restricted form of linguistic competence as peculiarly important to deciding about mental states has a long history. It is appropriate to wonder if this isn't taking too narrow a view.

I once was involved in a long discussion about the adequacy of the Turing Test and the soundness of Searle's argument. The discussion took place on an electronic network service (called Usenet) rather than in person.[12] For those who are unfamiliar with this sort of thing, one "posts" a message, which is relayed by telephone to other network sites where it can be read by anyone who is interested. These people can then post their replies, which are in turn circulated around, and the discussion is propagated. At one point, I was accused of inconsistency. How could I question the adequacy of the Turing Test when the very electronic medium that we were using closely resembled it? Wasn't I attributing all manner of mental states to my interlocutors simply in virtue of exchanging typed texts with them?

Indeed I was, but only because a number of other presumptions were already firmly in place. It was (and is) part of my general knowledge that there are no programs that come close to passing the Turing Test, much less engaging in philosophical discourse. The very idea of a test presupposes some plausible doubt in the matter. Where there was no doubt, I could not be said to be testing anyone. The same reply goes to those who claim that we are always Turing Testing each other in our everyday interactions. This is false, unless we employ a much looser and vaguer sense of the Turing Test than what Turing himself had in mind.

If the Turing Test is not penetrating enough to determine whether a system understands Chinese or anything else, what would be? What is involved in human understanding beyond the manipulation of texts? Although we shall look into these matters in more detail in the next chapter, a few points are salient.

---

12.   I thank my Usenet interlocutors, Jim Balter, Paul Torek, and Michael Ellis, for their insight and candor. I hope that I may someday meet them!

A great deal of what we call understanding is grounded in experience. We don't just understand language; we understand what is said *in* language, and we do so at least partly in virtue of having the right kinds of experiences. That we are the sorts of beings who can do this is surely not incidental to our understanding of language. Linguistic meaning is grounded in nonlinguistic experience. This is how language acquires a semantics.

Searle writes,

> The fact that the programmer and the interpreter of the computer output use the symbols to stand for objects in the world is totally beyond the scope of the computer. The computer, to repeat, has a syntax but no semantics.[13]

We have already seen that a token in a computer's memory is only a "symbol" in virtue of its having a meaning assigned to it by a person. Tokens are just objects; symbols are objects that have content, meaning, or reference. They are *about* something. This "aboutness" is called *intentionality* by philosophers. The numbers that appear in the display window of your pocket calculator refer to your bank balance only because you are using them for that purpose. Their intentionality is derived from yours. They refer because you mean them to. But what is it for *you* to mean or refer in that way? Your intentionality is apparently not derived. Your mental states do not refer to things simply in virtue of being used for that purpose by someone else. Their intentionality is somehow intrinsic to you. How is nonderived or intrinsic intentionality possible?

This is one of the central questions in contemporary philosophy of mind. There is much dispute not only about how intrinsic intentionality is possible but whether it exists at all and, if it does, what sort of thing it is. I cannot give it a full treatment here, but what I said above seems relevant. Understanding (an intentional state) a language presupposes some mode of mapping between a system's linguistic and nonlinguistic processes. For this even to be possible it must be capable of *having* nonlinguistic processes. The Turing Test itself says nothing of whether

---

13.   Searle, "Minds, Brains, and Programs," p. 370.

the system is even capable of any mode of nonlinguistic processing. I use the word "processing" instead of "experience" here so as not to complicate the matter any further by forcing the question of which processes are experiences. The difficulty of that question will be discussed in the next chapter.

A natural move at this point is to equip our Turing Test–passing computer with some sensory and motor peripherals. Let it perceive the world and interact with it, and let its interactions form and update the data structures that it uses to generate its clever Turing Test–passing texts. In short, let it be a robot and not just a computer in a box in a room. Searle considers this possibility, which he calls the "Robot Reply":

> Suppose we put a computer inside a robot, and this computer would not just take in formal symbols as input and give out formal symbols as output, but rather it would actually operate the robot in such a way that the robot does something very much like perceiving, walking, moving about, hammering nails, eating, drinking—anything you like. The robot would, for example, have a television camera attached to it that enabled it to see, it would have arms and legs that enabled it to act, and all of this would be controlled by its computer brain. Such a robot would . . . have genuine understanding and other mental states.[14]

He considers this possibility as a counterargument to his own position, but goes on to reject it. The robot, according to Searle, is in no better position to understand Chinese than its room-bound predecessor.

> Suppose that instead of the computer inside the robot, you put me inside the room and you give me again, as in the original Chinese case, more Chinese symbols with more instructions in English for matching Chinese symbols to Chinese symbols and feeding back Chinese symbols to the outside. Suppose unknown to me, some of the Chinese symbols that come to me come from a television camera attached to the robot, and other Chinese symbols that I am giving out serve to make the motors inside the robot move the robot's legs or

---

14.   Ibid., p. 362.

arms. It is important to emphasize that all I am doing is manipulating formal symbols: I know none of these other facts.[15]

There are some odd things about Searle's rebuttal of the Robot Reply. First, he depicts the tokens coming in from the sensors and those going out to the limbs as more "Chinese symbols," just like the Chinese symbols involved in the original scenario. This is certainly a mistake, and it appears to overlook something crucial. When you hear a voice speaking English you are first of all hearing sound, just as you are hearing sound when you listen to surf crashing on the beach. The spoken English is message-bearing sound; it consists of symbols. The surf noise is just sound. One of the first things that your brain must do is separate the message-bearing sound from all the other sounds, the background noise.[16] It sorts the auditory input into language and nonlanguage. How things go from there to constitute understanding is still unknown, but I cannot believe that that first step is insignificant. Searle's remark misses it altogether.

The second odd thing about Searle's rebuttal is that it misses the point that even if sensorimotor capabilities are not sufficient for understanding, they are surely at least necessary. Since the Turing Test does not test for these capabilities, the Robot Reply is actually another argument against the adequacy of the Turing Test.

Psychologist Steven Harnad has developed this line of argument, as in the following passage:

> Who is to say that the Turing Test, whether conducted in Chinese or in any other language, could be successfully passed without operations that draw on our sensory, motor, and other higher cognitive capacities as well? Where does the capacity to comprehend Chinese begin and the rest of our mental competence leave off? Searle has made the implicit assumption here—one that he shares with his

---

15.   Ibid.

16.   Of course, another possibility is that you are listening intently to the surf sounds and someone's talking is the background noise. The ability to shift background and foreground is yet another subtle aspect of our cognitive repertoire that we take for granted.

opponents in AI!—that there could exist a self-sufficient "module" that was able to pass his purely verbal Turing Test without simultaneously being able to do *everything else* we can do, i.e., without also being able to pass the Total Turing Test.[17]

The Total Turing Test tests the full range of capabilities, not just the ability to generate appropriate texts. Its use suggests a form of behaviorism, except it does not require reducing the meaning of statements about mental states to statements about behavior. Harnad dubs his theory "robotic functionalism." An important part of the theory is that the sort of processing that could plausibly explain mental states is not properly "symbolic" processing at all. We shall return to this idea in Chapter 6.

This is by no means the end of the responses to Searle or to strong AI. To some extent, the next two chapters are continuations of the responses to Searle. The Chinese Room is never, it seems, quite closed. Instead, it represents a core problem, and it is to Searle's credit that he has zeroed in on what is most *philosophically* problematic in AI. A deeper and more careful consideration of the strengths and weaknesses of some points of his argument will have to wait until we have clarified some other issues pertaining to mind and language. In particular, we need a more precise vocabulary for talking about intelligence and other mental properties. To that task we turn in the next chapter.

---

17. Steven Harnad, "Minds, Machines and Searle," *Journal of Experimental and Theoretical Artificial Intelligence,* 1, no. 1 (1989), 8–9. (ms.)

Chapter 5

The Nature of Intelligence

When artificial intelligence is discussed by laypersons, it is usually taken for granted that intelligence itself is relatively well understood. It is often assumed that intelligence is a unitary concept, embodying some single coherent meaning, even though it may not be completely understood. In fact, intelligence is anything but a unitary concept. The word "intelligence" is quite vague, encompassing a wide range of human and nonhuman capabilities, talents, and performances. Many workers in AI are aware of this vagueness and, in their research, single out one or more precise aspects of intelligence to attempt to model. This approach has its own difficulties, as we shall see later. But this point is often overlooked in philosophical discussions of artificial intelligence. The purpose of this chapter is to disambiguate the word "intelligence" and to discuss the possibilities of, and obstacles to, artificial realizations of the various aspects of intelligence.

In 1972 Hubert Dreyfus, a philosopher at the University of California at Berkeley, wrote a book called *What Computers Can't Do.*[1] This book enraged many workers in AI, including philosophers working in the field. It has become something of a classic in the literature, if only because so many people felt compelled to respond to Dreyfus's arguments. I shall adopt a less polemical tone in this chapter, but I shall cover some of the same ground that Dreyfus covered and make explicit reference to his ideas. Dreyfus was at great pains to sort out the many aspects

---

1. *What Computers Can't Do,* 2nd ed. (New York: Harper & Row, 1979).

of intelligence and to emphasize the extent to which these distinguish-able aspects are woven together and interdependent. The crux of Dreyfus's argument is that there is little reason to expect success in artificially implementing this or that bit of human intelligence without also implementing the rest of it. He argued that you cannot even in principle separate our ability to use language, to take one very signifi-cant example, from our ability to recognize and interact cognitively and emotionally with other human beings or from our ability to orient ourselves spatially and temporally. Human intelligence, on this view, is very much a package deal. This constitutes a possibly decisive objection to AI's modular approach, in which intelligence is approached as a set of interdependent—but essentially independent—functional modules. Hand in glove with AI's modular research strategy is the "modularity thesis" about the mind itself, which we shall also consider later in this chapter.

Tasks and Intelligence

Which requires most intelligence—playing a strong game of chess, "get-ting" a joke, or recognizing a person who walks into the room? Many of us would immediately reply that the chess game requires the most intelligence. After all, even very unintelligent people can tell and appre-ciate jokes, and a dog is perfectly capable of recognizing a person who enters the room.

So, in one sense of "intelligence," it takes hardly any intelligence at all to recognize people, but a considerable level is needed to play a good chess game. Yet of the three tasks mentioned, chess playing has turned out to be by far the easiest to implement artificially. The best of the current generation of chess-playing computers can beat all but the best human players. In contrast to this success, there has been some modest success in developing face-recognition programs, although there is still a long way to go. Artificial humor remains unexplored territory.

It would not be much of an exaggeration to say that the hardest tasks to implement by artificial intelligence are the very tasks that people can do without even thinking: recognizing faces (even after long absences), finding one's way around, speaking and understanding language. Why should these things be such difficult challenges to AI? Why is chess playing, if not exactly an *easy* programming task, an approachable AI problem? Clearly, chess playing and face recognition involve very different kinds of intelligence. What is different about them?

Chess

Chess is a game in which clearly identifiable pieces are moved around on a board according to a small set of unambiguous rules. If this sounds familiar, it should, because chess is not only a game but also a formal system. Like all formal systems, it is digital in that the tokens that are manipulated are unambiguously identifiable. A rook is a rook and not a pawn, and so forth; a chess set in which the pieces are not clearly and definitely distinguishable is useless. Each board position is a discrete state.

The rules by which the chess pieces are moved are completely unambiguous and exhaustive; they cover all situations. There is no situation that can arise in a chess game that requires a "judgment call" as to the legality of the move involved. Using the language of formal systems, we can say that there is an effective method for determining the legality of any chess move and an effective method for determining whether the game is over and who, if anybody, has won. The aspect of the game of chess that is not yet capable of being understood as a formal system is the strategic aspect of the game, the goal-directed choice of moves to produce a win. At any given stage of a chess game there are one or more (usually about thirty) legal moves possible. Choosing the best move means choosing the move that is most likely to lead to a win.

The game of chess can be understood as a branching tree of possible board positions. You begin with the pieces set up on the board in the standard manner, and each legal move results in a new configuration of pieces on the board. In response to each possible move there are many possible legal moves, and in response to each of them there are many more possible moves. Thought of in this way, from the very first move of a game of chess there is a path of moves that leads to a win, a loss, a stalemate, or a draw. The strategy of winning a game of chess amounts to selecting a path that leads only to winning configurations. Every chess game is a path through this tree of branching possibilities. It follows that there are only finitely many possible chess games. Although the number is finite, it is a fantastically large number, somewhere in the neighborhood of 10^{120} possible games. Because this number is so large, it is not an option simply to examine the entire branching tree of possible chess games, pick out in advance only the winning paths through that tree, and use that information in an effective method for winning at chess. This approach *is* a possibility for much simpler games, such as tic-tac-toe. A computer programmed to play tic-tac-toe can work out a complete game tree and then follow a move path that leads to winning positions, or at least does not lead to any losing positions.

The tic-tac-toe example illustrates another point, namely that even though it may be in principle possible to construct a complete game tree, it does not follow that the use of that game tree provides an effective method for winning. Even though a computer may be able to generate such a game tree for tic-tac-toe, the computer does not necessarily win every game. Against an even moderately clever human opponent, most games will end in a draw. The computer will never lose a game of tic-tac-toe, however; the game tree gives it enough information to avoid a loss in every case.

It is not known at this time whether it is even in principle possible to develop an effective method for winning chess. Such a method would involve developing an algorithm for every possible situation that would lead only to winning positions. There are people who believe that the player of the white pieces, who has the first move, has a sufficient advantage to "force" a win. If the complete game tree for chess could be examined, it would be possible to prove or disprove this conjecture. Since this is a practical impossibility, however, it remains a conjecture until and unless some other means of testing it can be found. Since a win cannot even be forced by the player who moves first in a game of tic-tac-toe, it strikes me as unlikely that the first player in chess can do so, but that, too, is only a suspicion of mine; the required proof is still lacking.

Getting the computer simply to *play* according to the rules of chess, then, is a matter of representing one formal system, namely the rules of chess, in terms of another formal system, in this case a computer programming language. The computer programming language is a formal system designed to make it easy for human beings to get a digital computer to do useful things in yet another formal system, the digital token-manipulation system of the physical machine itself. Getting the computer to play a strong, or winning, game of chess presents an additional set of problems, in the absence of a decisive winning algorithm. Basically, the way this is managed is to have the computer search as much of the game tree as it is capable of searching within reasonable time constraints.[2] If at any given point in the game there are on the average thirty possible moves, then for each move that the computer attempts to look ahead into the game tree the number of possible board configurations to be examined increases by a factor of thirty. So, if the computer is to look ahead five moves (taking a "move" to be the manipulation of one piece by one player, as opposed to a full move in which both players play), then the computer is going to have to examine about 30^5 board positions. This is quite a large number, over 24 million, to look at. But the question remains, if these board positions are not end-of-game positions—for which there is an effective method for determining win, loss, or draw—what is the computer looking for when it examines them? There is an effective method for determining whether a position is a win or a loss, but is there an effective method for determining whether a given board position is "good" or "bad"?

There is no such effective method, so the programmer must fall back on a set of *heuristics*. Heuristics are strategic principles of demonstrated usefulness. In the course of many chess games, we have learned that if you can capture many of the opponent's pieces without losing many of your own pieces, this increases the likelihood that you will eventually be able to get to a winning position. It is not necessarily the case that you will win, because there are situations in which you may lose even though you have a considerable material advantage over your opponent. But, other

---

2. For example, within the time limits imposed in tournament chess.

things being equal, it seems to be a good idea to capture your opponent's pieces. So this is one heuristic that can be programmed. As the program searches various board configurations to a given depth in the game tree, it can look for outcomes in which it is able to capture pieces. It will also look for other kinds of advantages that it can produce, such as advantageous positions, checks against the king, threats, pins, and other tactics. The strength of the game that the computer will play obviously depends upon the reliability of the heuristics used in the program, which in turn depends upon the programmer's ability to identify useful heuristics and to represent them in a programming language. Another way to put this would be as follows: The programmer needs to develop an algorithm that captures the experienced chess player's *judgment*.

Of these two aspects of programming computers to play chess—translating the rules of the game into a formal language and translating the experienced player's judgment into a set of programmable heuristics—the latter is by far the more difficult task. The reason for this brings us to a point that has general application to appreciating the difficulty of programming various aspects of intelligence. The point is that while some forms of intelligent activity are *explicit,* and therefore readily captured by algorithms, others are *tacit,* to use the terms of the philosopher Michael Polanyi. In his works, Polanyi distinguished tacit knowledge and explicit knowledge as follows: Explicit knowledge is just that knowledge of which an account can be given, which can be verbalized. What we know explicitly is what we can say how we know. Tacit knowledge, on the other hand, is knowledge that we use constantly, but without being able quite to say how we know what we know, or even exactly what it is that we do know. We have explicit knowledge of the rules of the game of chess, if we know how to play the game at all. They are not really that complicated. But when an experienced player makes a move, she may not be able to give any very complete and articulated reason for that move, rather than some other move, other than to mention some general principles of play.[3] When asked how they make

---

3. Of course, there are many situations in which she would be able to tell you *exactly* why she made the move she made.

their decisions, most master chess players reply that they rely upon their accumulated experience and study. They favor certain moves because the board positions that result from those moves are similar to board positions that they have encountered or studied before and that they feel put them in a strong position for a win. They might not be able to tell you, however, the exact sequence of moves that would lead to that win. The master chess player does not evaluate millions of board positions in her head before making a move. The computer does, because at this time this is the only way that we know to get a computer to play a creditable game of chess. Since the knowledge that a master chess player has that enables him or her to play a strong game of chess remains partially tacit, the programmer must rely on those few principles of strategy and tactics that can be made explicit, and hope that those heuristics, in conjunction with a superhuman ability to examine large numbers of board positions, will result in a win for the computer. So far, this approach to chess programming has worked rather well. There is some dispute about whether it will eventually produce programmed computers that can win against all human opponents. As computer hardware becomes more sophisticated, the computers are capable of searching more and more deeply into the game tree, and therefore evaluating ever larger numbers of board positions within a given time. It seems to me that at some point the sheer brute force of this approach will overwhelm all human challengers, but the field is still open.

There is another line of argument that says that while the computer may simulate playing the game of chess, it's not really playing chess. A real game of chess, the argument continues, is a contest of wills between two players who care about the outcome. The computer, no matter how powerful and impressive its performance may be, is still just performing millions of computations in a very short span of time and in a completely deterministic way. There is no way that this computational process can be the same thing as the purposive commitment of a human player striving to defeat another human player. The point of this argument, of course, is that whatever it is that we humans do when we play chess must be something quite different from the mere manipulation of tokens in a formal system. While some of what we are doing when we play chess may indeed involve a process in our brains that might be described as token-manipulation in a formal system,[4] surely chess playing is more than just that. Though it may be useful and even fun to play a game against a computer simulation, it is not the real thing. This argument insists that the simulation of a process can never be collapsed into or confused with the realization of that process. It involves the further interesting suggestion that to be engaged in a mental activity, as opposed to merely simulating that activity, presupposes that one also knows that one is engaged in that activity. To play chess, one must know that one is playing chess, and it is precisely this that the programmed computer cannot possibly "know."

This objection, of course, is quite different from the objection that Poe had, which had to do with the possibility of even executing a proper game of chess. Some will complain that this objection is a mere semantic quibble about what a game of chess "really" is. If you want to define chess as a *human* activity, then of course no computer can play it. But there is no reason, say the critics of this argument, to define chess as a particularly human activity when it can be defined in purely formal terms. The critics may be right. It does seem desperate to insist that "real" chess is played by committed antagonists. Still, this argument alerts us to yet another dimension of the disputes in the philosophy of artificial intelligence: the extent to which the theory and technology of computing are redefining concepts, getting us to think of more and more things as formal systems. It is possible that it *matters* whether we think of our activities and ourselves as formal systems or as something else. This topic is examined in more detail in the last chapter.

Recognition

Recognition tasks present formidable difficulties for artificial intelligence. The sheer range of recognition tasks that we are able to perform with little or no effort is quite impressive. For example, we are easily able

---

4. But even this is controversial. The brain may not be a discrete-state system at all.

to recognize the faces of people whom we know, even people whom we have only met a few times. What is more striking is the fact that we are able to recognize faces even after long periods of time when the individuals involved may have undergone numerous and significant changes. Anyone who has been to a class reunion after ten or fifteen years has experienced this. People gain weight, lose weight, grow beards, change hairstyles and hair color—through it all we are able to do a very good job of recognizing them. We don't do a perfect job, of course; it does happen that we fail to recognize people as well, but all things considered, our ability to recognize faces is remarkable.

Our powers of recognition are not strictly visual either. The telephone rings and within seconds you recognize the voice at the other end even though it may be somebody whom you haven't heard from for many years. And even though the human ability to discriminate odors and tastes is in many cases not as highly developed as it is in other species, we do a fair job of recognizing with these senses as well.

To consider a single example of human recognition ability, consider the ability to read different forms of writing. This includes printed writing in a variety of fonts as well as human handwriting. Although we may fail when it comes to certain handwriting specimens, on the whole we are astonishingly successful at deciphering the written word regardless of a wide range of possible variations in its appearance. Douglas Hofstadter wrote an essay in which he discussed the variety of ways in which the letter A is represented, and the difficulty of the task of programming a computer just to recognize it.

It is tempting to consider recognition to be a task that simply involves some elaborate form of matching. Given an input stimulus, either visual or acoustic, perhaps we simply record it and "look it up" in a stored table of some sort in memory. If we find a match, then the recognition is accomplished. If we don't find a match, there is no recognition. Something of the sort was contemplated by Plato in the *Theaetetus* over two thousand years ago. Even the simpleminded matching model of recognition faces some serious difficulties. For example, in order for anything at all to be recognized according to this theory, a template of some sort must be stored in memory, and anything that is not stored as a template cannot be recognized. So when you see a face, some mechanism in your brain must attempt to match the image that it sees against every one in a long list of stored face templates, until a match is found or until the end of the list is reached. But most forms of recognition are accomplished almost instantaneously, whereas this lookup and matching procedure would certainly be time-consuming. Moreover, there is an even more fundamental objection to simple matching as a model for recognition tasks: This model could only explain those cases where what we see matches exactly what we have seen before, or where what we hear matches exactly what we have heard before. It cannot explain the class-reunion case, where we see a face that is drastically altered but nevertheless immediately recognizable, or the voice that is different yet somehow the same. Nor can it explain how we are able to read the handwriting of someone whose handwriting we have never seen before.

Can the matching model be extended and made more sophisticated to account for these recognition tasks? Let's consider how this might be done. It could be that what is stored, in the case of facial recognition, is not a literal template of the face but a record of certain "essential characteristics" of the face. If this is so, then when we see an individual later we do not attempt to match the perceived face against the stored image detail for detail, but rather we look only for the essential characteristics. This theory allows for wide variation in the nonessential characteristics of the object to be recognized. The problem with this theory is that it requires an additional theory concerning what characteristics of an object are essential and what characteristics are nonessential for recognition. Furthermore, an additional theory is needed that stipulates the permissible range of transformations that the essential characteristics can be subject to. Even the essential characteristics need not be invariant for recognition to take place.

These caveats should not be taken to mean that the template model of recognition is impossible to implement. It may turn out to be the only game in town. The difficulties involved in producing recognition algorithms, however, are formidable. There is some evidence that a connectionist—as opposed to algorithmic—approach to recognition will be more successful. Connectionism, mentioned briefly in Chapter 1, is the subject of the next chapter.

Speech recognition is another area in which a great deal of research in artificial intelligence has been done and continues to be done. The problems in speech recognition are analogous to the problems in other forms of recognition. Human beings are able to recognize and understand utterances in their own language that they have never heard before despite wide variations in accent, pronunciation, tempo of speech, pitch changes, and vocal characteristics. We recognize speech instantaneously, or close to it. AI has had modest success in programming speech recognition. There are programs that are capable of understanding a small range of utterances, if those utterances are spoken clearly by people whose vocal characteristics fall within some predetermined range of variation. In the early days of AI, it was widely believed that it would not take terribly long to develop machines capable of translating spoken utterances directly into printed text of some sort, thus eliminating the need for keyboards. This technology is still a long way off, precisely because we now understand that the task of speech recognition involves much more than coding the input sounds in some manner and matching them against stored representations. In fact, research in cognitive psychology has revealed to us that human beings actually hear only about 70 percent of what is said to them; the remaining 30 percent doesn't register at all. In the case of telephone conversation, this percentage is even lower. This does not present a serious obstacle to human speech recognition, however, because our ability to recognize speech is intimately connected with our ability to understand it. There is now good reason to believe that speech recognition involves, in addition to the simple recognition of sound sequences, the ability to reconstruct what the meaning must be in the context in which the utterance is heard. If this is correct, then the task of speech recognition cannot even in principle be separated from the task of speech understanding.

To return to the domain of chess playing for just a moment, some interesting research has revealed that, contrary to popular belief, chess masters do not have prodigious memories. Their memories are not significantly better than anyone else's. When asked to memorize the positions of pieces in random chessboard configurations, they do no better than novices to the game. Where the differences emerge is when the board positions to be memorized are not random but taken from actual chess game situations. In this case, the chess masters' ability to remember board positions is very highly developed. In other words, their ability to remember and recognize board positions depends upon those board positions being meaningful to them. To a novice player, one configuration of pieces is about as good as any other; the novice has not built up a "semantic network" in which to categorize the board positions that he sees. That is, they don't mean much to him; they are not linked in his understanding to any other chess situations or outcomes. The chess master has developed such a network and uses it to good advantage in memory and recognition tasks.

If this line of thinking is correct, then recognition may be understood as a species of, or perhaps an aspect of, understanding itself. Our ability to recognize things is closely linked to and interdependent with our ability to make sense of them, to position them in some kind of logical or semantic space, to cope with them. These faculties of understanding may in turn only make sense against a backdrop of interests, commitments, desires, fears, and other aspects of involvement in the world. It may be that the hypothetical speech-recognition transcriber may not only have to understand what is said to it but will also have to care.

There is a further line of difficulties that have to do with engineering considerations. Modern digital computers operate at very high speeds. As was mentioned in a previous chapter, even modest digital computing equipment now available is capable of performing millions of operations per second. The human brain, by contrast, is composed of interconnected neurons whose speed of operation is orders of magnitude slower than this. There are prototype facial-recognition programs in existence, but these programs, even running on high-speed computing equipment, may take many minutes to recognize a face from a stored bank of faces. Human beings operating with much slower neural equipment perform this task almost instantly, as previously mentioned. This suggests very strongly that whatever it is that the brain is doing is something quite different from what these digital computers are being programmed to do.[5]

One might respond that it doesn't really matter how the digital computer accomplishes what it does; what is important is that it does so. This assertion, which once again brings up one of the fundamental issues in the philosophy of artificial intelligence, needs to be considered very carefully. If we understand recognition to be a *mental* capability that human beings have, is it important that other systems should recognize things in the same way if they are to be said to possess this mental attribute? If we regard the mind simply as a collection of task-oriented modules, then clearly nothing important hinges on mimicking the specific actions of the human brain, other than questions of efficiency. If on the other hand we have an understanding of the mind according to which mental and biological characteristics interpenetrate and are interdependent, then clearly it will not be sufficient to stray too far from the concretely human details of the mental.

Language

In the chapter on the mind-body problem, I described how Descartes was impressed with the spectacle of the automata at the Royal Garden of Versailles. He was confident that a theory of biological motor function could be created along hydraulic lines, similar to the principles used in creating these automated figures. He was also quite confident that no automaton could ever possess truly mental characteristics, and the particular task that he thought would never be accomplished by a machine was the use of natural language. It would be fair to say that Descartes saw human language as the "mark of the mental." This way of looking at things is made especially attractive by the fact that natural language use seems to be a talent unique to human beings. Although other species of animals have systems of communication, only humans use what can properly be described as a language.

It is worth taking a moment, therefore, to distinguish language from

---

5. The chapter on connectionism takes this argument a bit further.

other communication systems. It is well known, for example, that certain species of birds may use one call as a mating call and another to announce the presence of a predator in the vicinity, and perhaps other calls for other specific functions. Why then do we not say that these birds have a language of calls? Similar systems of calls are found in abundance throughout the animal kingdom. Are we simply being chauvinistic in insisting that only humans have languages? Perhaps we are; it would not be the first time that human beings arrogated to themselves some special characteristics that set them apart from everything else in nature. In this case, we can point to one very important feature of human language that is apparently missing from other systems of animal communication. That feature is called *generativity*. If a given species of bird has a dozen distinct calls, then birds of that species can "say" exactly a dozen things. It is important to recognize the full implications of this fact. It follows, for example, that the number of messages that such a bird can utter is exactly equal to the size of its vocabulary. It also follows that the elements in that "vocabulary" are fully constituted messages—complete sentences, if you will.

By contrast, what human beings do with language is strikingly different. When we speak of a human being's vocabulary, we may be referring to some 20–30,000 words, for an average college student. Estimates vary. The elements of that vocabulary, what we call "words," are themselves subsentential units. Complete messages, or sentences, are composed by combining these units according to rules into larger strings. Consequently, while an individual's vocabulary may comprise 30,000 words, the number of sentences that that individual can utter is far larger than 30,000. In fact, it is potentially infinite. So the property that is called generativity by linguists is the property of a language by which its users are able to make combinations from a finite stock of elements to generate a potentially unlimited number of messages, or sentences.[6] It is also important to note the fact that generativity allows

---

6. The terms "message" and "sentence" are technically not interchangeable. A sentence is a grammatical construction, whereas a message is a semantic idea. It should be clear that there are many messages that one can convey without using grammatically complete or correct sentences. While such distinctions are important to linguists, they are not particularly significant in this context.

us to generate *new* sentences, sentences that we have never heard before and that we have never uttered before. In fact, we do this all the time and it doesn't pose the slightest difficulty in understanding. What a bird can "understand" is strictly limited to what is in its finite repertoire of calls. A bird cannot combine those calls by means of some sort of grammar to produce novel meanings or more complicated utterances. There is no clear evidence that any species other than human beings are capable of using the communication system in a generative way, which is the essence of language. As may be familiar to many readers, there has been some important and suggestive work done with chimpanzees using human sign language. According to some interpretations of this work, the chimpanzees have achieved a modest level of success in generating new utterances from the basic sign-language vocabulary that they have been taught. At this time, this work remains controversial; the experimental design has been subject to much criticism, and most regard the hypothesis as unproven.

Interestingly, what language has in common with other nonlinguistic forms of communication is semantic content. The sentences that we utter mean something and birdcalls mean something and the barking of a dog means something. Where they differ is in syntax. The generativity of language is only possible if there are specific rules of syntax. In an earlier chapter, we saw that the complete range of possibilities of a purely formal system can be specified entirely by means of syntactic rules, without any necessary semantic interpretation to the elements of that system, even though such an interpretation is normally what makes the system interesting and useful for humans in the long run. It is therefore natural to wonder at this point whether a natural language such as English or French is in fact a formal system. After all, the essence of a formal system is its syntactic structure. And the essence of what distinguishes a language from nonlinguistic communication is also its syntactic structure. It seems only natural to conclude that a natural language is a formal system used for communication among humans.

As it turns out, this conclusion is controversial. For one thing, no one has yet been able to enumerate a complete set of syntactic rules for any known natural language. That is, although we all seem to know in a rough-and-ready way what is and what isn't a sentence, no one has yet succeeded in representing in the form of completely unambiguous rules this knowledge that we all have. Despite a great deal of work, there is not yet an algorithm for distinguishing the grammatically legal sentences of English from the illegal sentences. Keep in mind that one of the requirements of a formal system is that there be an exhaustive set of rules for distinguishing the legal or well-formed strings from the illegal or ill-formed strings. Furthermore, all natural languages seem to tolerate a great deal of both semantic and syntactic improvisation. We not only coin new words and expressions on the spot, with a reasonable expectation of being understood as we do so, but we also use novel syntactic forms with an equal expectation of being understood. In fact, it is well known that human beings using natural language can do all kinds of violence to the accepted rules of grammar of that language without the slightest diminution of comprehensibility.

One response to this fact might be as follows: Since the grammar of the language is simply a description of how the language in fact works, it is not really possible that one can use the language while breaking a grammatical rule. When that appears to be happening, all that really shows is that what we thought were the rules in fact are not the rules and we need to formulate another set of rules. This response does underscore the fact that when we talk about the grammar of a language, we are not talking about a prescriptive set of rules or etiquette for using the language in a "correct way" that you might associate with your high-school English classes. We are rather referring to a complete scientific description of the regularities of that language. If some mode of expression works in the language, it necessarily follows that that mode of expression conforms to the true grammar of that language. Still, it must be conceded at this point that it's still a matter of conjecture whether any natural language has such a grammar in the sense that it would conform to the requirements of a formal system.

To summarize some of these observations about language, we may take note of the fact that even the least intelligent humans are capable of mastering a natural language to at least a modest level of proficiency. A severely retarded person may be able to speak quite passable English, although even a weak game of chess might be far beyond his powers. Despite vigorous attempts by theoretical linguists, no one has yet succeeded in demonstrating that any natural human language conforms to the requirements of a formal system. It should come as no surprise then that attempts to program computers to "understand" natural languages have met with only a very modest level of success.

I say that it should come as no surprise, but in fact when artificial intelligence was young, among the first and most enthusiastic predictions made by its enthusiasts was the prediction that it would not be long before digital computers would be capable of, for example, translating speeches and texts from one natural language to another. It was believed and hoped that they would soon put armies of translators out of work. All that would be necessary would be somehow to input the text in one language, feed the computer the appropriate translating program, and wait for the translated output. If language were a formal system whose elements and rules we had a complete theory of, then this is just what we would expect to be able to do. So in the early 1960s a flurry of work was done on the "natural-language problem." Many optimists believed that as the translation problem was solved, the interface problem would also be solved. That is, it would no longer be necessary to give computers instructions in the rigorous but somewhat awkward coding systems of the high-level programming languages. Instead a user might type in at the keyboard a friendly English instruction such as "Please look over my grade list for this semester and figure out the averages, distributions, deviations, and anything else that looks interesting. Print out the results." The computer, armed with a natural-language program, would understand these instructions and would itself translate them into some internal set of instructions and carry out the task without having to be told each little detail by a human programmer.

It didn't work out as expected. At a very early stage in the research, the scientists noted that it seems impossible to give a proper syntactic analysis of the structure of a sentence without taking into account the meanings assigned to the elements of that sentence. This just isn't the way it is supposed to be when you are dealing with a formal system. You are supposed to be able to look at the structure of the thing and analyze it into its fundamental units—to parse it, in other words—without any reference at all to the interpretation.

Here is a classic example of this problem. Consider the following two English sentences: "Time flies like an arrow. Fruit flies like a banana." The verb in the first sentence is "flies"; the verb in the second sentence is "like." A fluent speaker of English is able to understand these two sentences without any difficulty at all, and to do so instantly. To write an algorithm that is capable of discriminating the structural difference between these two sentences is something else again. Although the surface structure of the two sentences is closely parallel, it is obvious that the same rules cannot be applied to the two sentences in the same way. It is not difficult to come up with examples of this sort; in fact, natural languages seem to be saturated with them.

Such facts have led the linguist Noam Chomsky to suppose that if indeed natural language is a formal system, its regularities do not exist at the level of surface structures. There must be a "deep structure" underlying these surface structures that conforms to the principles of a formal system. Noting that children from all different cultures and linguistic environments seem to be able to acquire language—any language—at about the same rate and the same age, Chomsky concludes that there is a "universal grammar" common to all natural languages that acts as a constraint on the possible surface structures that learnable human languages may have. Since it seems that, while some languages are considerably more difficult than other languages for adults to learn as second languages, any human child can learn any human language with equal ease as a first language, Chomsky supposed that our knowledge of the universal grammar underlying all human languages is an innate endowment. The process that we call "learning a language" is really a matter of learning a set of transformation rules that allow us to map the surface structure of the language to which we are exposed as children onto the deep structure of the universal grammar with which we are innately acquainted. Although this isn't the place to undertake a detailed study of Chomsky's ground-breaking contributions to linguistics, two points do need to be made. First, neither Chomsky nor his followers have had a great deal of success in devising a theory of the universal grammar. That is, while there is no shortage of arguments that purport to demonstrate that there must be a universal grammar, to date rather little headway has been made in describing the concrete details of that grammar. Second, even if the universal grammar should someday be fully described, it does not follow that it will be of a form that can be represented in a purely formal system. As we know, a requirement of a formal system is that the elements within that system must be unambiguously identifiable tokens. This just may not be possible for the universal grammar of natural language, if there is such a thing. The research program that is based on the hypothesis that natural languages can be shown to be formal systems is called *computational linguistics*. For computational linguistics to work, it would have to be the case that in principle natural-language understanding can be logically and operationally separated from our other capacities. If it could be shown that, on the contrary, our ability to use language is an outgrowth and extension of other more or less biological abilities and involvements with the world, the picture would be much bleaker for computational linguistics. It is a question of how much of what humans are able to do we would have to enable a computer to do to get that computer to deal with natural language.

Although in these remarks I do not attempt to conceal my skepticism concerning computational linguistics, I have to remind the reader that the case is far from closed. These are vital areas of research, and at the present time there is simply too much that we don't understand about what language is and how we use it. My skepticism is as conjectural as the computational linguist's optimism.

Modularity can be a powerful strategy for humans who face complex tasks. What modularity essentially amounts to is the strategy of breaking those complex tasks down, or analyzing them into logically independent but smaller and more manageable tasks or modules. The problem of programming a computer to play chess can be broken down into the problem of writing rules for how a rook moves, how a pawn moves, when a king is in check, and so on. The fact that this is a powerful strategy for humans doesn't mean, however, that nature and evolution have followed the same strategy in designing us. It seems to me to be a mistake to suppose that all of nature must be written in the language that we prefer to read.

Consciousness and Sentience

So far, in this chapter dealing with the nature and variety of human intelligence, I've said nothing about consciousness. Yet there are some who would say that consciousness is the single most essential and important fact about intelligence, or at least about the mind. What is needed, then, is an account of the relation that exists between consciousness, intelligence, and the mental. It is to be expected that such an account will draw some lines through this territory that may strike some as arbitrary. This is so because these concepts are so seldom carefully distinguished that the language of consciousness, intelligence, and mind is somewhat blurry. One of the principal tasks of philosophy is to explore these vaguely marked-out territories and, when possible, to do some surveying and make the boundaries at least somewhat clearer. The price of such clarity is inevitably that the surveyed territory looks a bit different than it did before the surveying took place. We may expect that this will be no exception.

The first thing to notice about consciousness is that it is very difficult to say precisely what it is. It is such a central fact of the human condition that it is difficult and perhaps impossible to explain it in terms that are any more intelligible than consciousness itself. To the extent that explanations involve describing the less familiar in terms of the more familiar, what could be more familiar than consciousness?[7] The philosopher Peter Unger stated the matter as follows:

> Without meaning to be doctrinaire, we might very roughly express our working stance like this: if you are (sometimes) conscious, then you already know what consciousness is, even if you can't say much about what you thus know; if an entity is never conscious, then there is nothing useful to be said to that entity in this matter.[8]

---

7.   There is also some controversy about whether this model of explanation is sufficiently general to cover all of the things that we count as explanations. To take one very notable example, scientific explanations of everyday phenomena are often couched in terms that are considerably less familiar than the phenomena that they purport to explain.

8.   Peter Unger, "Consciousness and Self-Identity," in *Midwest Studies in Philosophy*, X: *Studies in the Philosophy of Mind*, eds. Peter French, Theodore E. Uehling, Jr., and Howard K. Wettstein, (Minneapolis: University of Minnesota Press, 1986), p. 63.

Still, a few general observations can be made. The words "consciousness" and "experience" mark off roughly the same processes in nature. That is, those processes that we would call experiences are precisely the processes of which we are conscious. If some version of the token-token identity theory is true, then we may say that some but certainly not all processes that occur in the central nervous system of human beings are experiences. Obviously, there are many such processes occurring at every moment that are not experiences; we are not conscious of most of what is going on in our nervous system. So to be conscious is just to be in a state or to be undergoing a process that is either identical with, or somehow associated with, experience. That such states and processes occur in the human nervous system is a matter on which there is no doubt. What is more controversial is whether such states and processes can occur in man-made systems, such as digital computers.

To the extent that it is plausible to attribute consciousness to the nonhuman animals, it is also plausible to say that those animals have experiences. This is not, of course, to say that the experiences that other animals have are similar in every detail to the experiences that human beings have. It is simply to note a clear commonality. Even though I have only the behavior of other animals on which to base my supposition, and even though, as we shall soon see, this may not be the most secure basis for such a supposition, I nevertheless find it implausible to assert that only human beings have experiences. Descartes, as we have already seen, did assert just that: that despite appearances, the nonhuman species of animals are simply biological machines without any associated consciousness. Descartes' argument was that mankind's linguistic abilities demonstrated that only humans have consciousness. I shall adduce some evidence in this section to show that Descartes' argument was unfounded. For the time being, then, I shall assume that consciousness and experience are not limited to human beings.

Subjectivity and Bats

Some time ago, the philosopher Thomas Nagel wrote a paper entitled "What Is It Like to Be a Bat?" This paper stirred a fair amount of controversy because in it Nagel attempted to show how the fact of consciousness is both central and irreducible to any other facts. He develops these ideas in greater detail in his more recent book *The View from Nowhere*. Nagel's idea is that conscious beings or systems are not just objects in the world, although they are undoubtedly at least that, but are also *subjects*. That is, they are the subjects of experience. To be the subject of experience is to have a certain point of view on the world. This idea of subjectivity is absolutely central to the human experience of reality. The problem is that when we attempt to explain things, we adopt a stance that has come to be called "objectivity." In being objective, we attempt to subtract from our account of a phenomenon all of the features of it that depend upon a particular point of view. The scientific explanation of the fact that water expands when it freezes into ice, for example, does not make any reference to what this process is like to you or to me or to anybody. Instead, it purports to describe the process as it is in itself, apart from anybody's point of view. Nagel dubbed this objective way of looking at things "the view from nowhere."

Nagel's now-famous phrase is that subjectivity is "what it is like to be something." If the bat has experiences, then a bat is conscious and is the subject of those experiences. If so, then there is something that it is like to be a bat. If a bicycle is not the subject of any experiences, then it is not conscious, and therefore it is not like anything to be a bicycle. In the context of the philosophy of artificial intelligence, we might ask is it like anything to be a programmed digital computer, or a programmed Turing Test–passing digital computer? More precisely, we can distinguish the question, *Might* it be like anything to be a Turing Test–passing digital computer from the question, *Must* it be like anything to be a Turing Test–passing digital computer? If Nagel is right, we cannot hope to find an objective answer to those questions, because in adopting the mode of objectivity, subjectivity is precisely what we subtract from the picture of the world. What it is like to be something is just not a part of the objective description of the world.

Science has shown objectivity to be a powerful tool, capable of putting man in a position to transcend the limitations of particular viewpoints.

In attempting to be objective, I am trying to get beyond the way things seem to me. I am trying to get at the way things are in themselves. But if there are any facts about the world that are inextricably linked to the way things seem to me, then those facts are necessarily going to be left out of my objective version of the way the world is. If these reflections are on the mark, and if a modern philosophy of artificial intelligence aspires to scientific objectivity, then it would appear to follow that an objective account of the possibility, or impossibility, of artificial consciousness or artificial experience must lie forever beyond philosophy's grasp.

Not everyone would accept Nagel's account of the matter, however. In fact, many have accused him of a kind of mysticism when it comes to confronting consciousness and experience. Nagel's critics argue that if materialism is correct, then consciousness must arise from some set of processes within the nervous system. If we can but come to understand those processes, then we will have a handle on how it is that certain physical systems can also be conscious systems and can therefore be the subjects of experiences. Coming to understand those physical processes will allow us to enlarge our objective picture of the world sufficiently to include consciousness and subjectivity within it. Nagel can be seen as countering that, even if we knew in microscopic detail every facet of the operation of the nervous system of human beings and other animals, we still would not be in a position to say what it is to be conscious, or in virtue of what those particular states of the nervous system are conscious states and processes. We might be in a position to draw a detailed map of correlations between brain states and conscious states, but we still would not have explained how there comes to be consciousness in the world at all. At some point, Nagel contends, consciousness is simply an irreducible brute fact about nature.[9]

Qualia and Rainbows

There is yet another aspect to the puzzle of consciousness and subjectivity. The details of our consciousness of the world have a certain

---

9.   If he is right, it is not just a difficulty for AI, but for any attempt to explain the mind by physicalist principles.

character, a certain identity. Things appear a certain way to us. The way in which things appear to us is difficult to capture by means of a purely objective account. The particular ways in which the world appears to a particular subject of experience are called *qualia* (singular: *quale*).

A famous philosophical puzzle about qualia is the *inverted-spectrum problem*. Imagine two individuals, Alice and Beth, who are alike in every way but one: their perception of certain colors. We may suppose that Alice has the "normal" way of perceiving colors. That is, the word "green" denotes for her a certain perceived quality of objects, the same quality that you and I associate with the word "green." You and I and Alice experience that quale of green when we look at such things as grass and leaves. For Beth, however, things are different. When she looks at grass or leaves she also experiences a certain quale. But the quale she experiences is the one that we associate with the word "red." Since she has been this way since birth, she has learned to call grass and leaves green and she has no idea that what she is experiencing is a different quale from what you and I and Alice experience when we look at grass and leaves. But when Beth looks at apples and roses and fire engines, although she calls these objects "red," the quale that she experiences is in fact just the same quale that you and I and Alice experience as green. In short, the red and green bands of Beth's subjective spectrum are inverted.

The first thing to note about this little thought experiment is that it seems to make perfect sense. That is, it doesn't present any conceptual difficulties to the understanding. You know just what I mean when I state that the red and green bands of Beth's subjective spectrum are inverted. In fact, I probably could have stated the problem in significantly more compact terms than what I used. I was striving for a certain level of precision in order to make philosophical sense of the problem, not to make it easier to understand on the first pass.

The next thing that might occur to you is that while it presents no special difficulties to say how it is that Beth is different from Alice, it is less easy to say how we might identify Beth, or indeed discover if there are any people like Beth in the real world. It obviously would not do to ask them what color a rose or a lawn appears to be, because such people would give just the same answers that you or I would give. In fact, how do you and I know that we are not experiencing inverted spectra from each other? There doesn't seem to be any way that we could find out by simply talking about our experiences. It doesn't help matters to point out a lot of details about the wavelengths of the various visible colors of light. Even if we could give a rich and microprecise account of the wavelengths of light impinging upon Beth's retina and the precise neural impulses delivered via her optic nerve to her optical cortex and a precise account of the entire gamut of cortical activity that results in her saying "that's green," we still would not be in a position to say what qualia she is experiencing at that particular moment. That is, we can easily conceive of all of the objective details being just what they are but the experienced qualia being something quite different.

The inverted-spectrum problem seems to support Nagel's point that there is something essentially missing from the objective description of things. The inverted-spectrum problem is a problem of subjectivity, and therefore it makes no sense from the standpoint of objectivity. Objectively, we cannot say how it is that Beth is different from you and me. Objectively, Beth utters the same things that we utter when confronted with the same stimuli. According to her, roses are red and grass is green.

We may think of it in this way: If we had an objective understanding of the inverted-spectrum problem, we would know how to program two artificially intelligent computers in such a way that their subjective spectra would differ in precisely the same way that Alice's and Beth's subjective spectra differ. If we cannot do so, but nevertheless insist that there is a real difference between Alice and Beth, then we have to concede that our programs have failed to capture a real distinction between the mental characteristics of Alice and Beth. It seems fair to say that a complete theory of the mind ought to make sense of that distinction, and that a proper computer realization of mind ought to be based on a complete theory. If so, then the inverted spectrum problem lies at the heart, and not at the fringe, of the philosophy of artificial intelligence.

Intelligence without Consciousness

So far, it has seemed to make sense to talk about intelligence in terms of capacity to perform certain tasks, such as language use, chess-playing and face-recognition. Consciousness, on the other hand, has been talked about without any explicit reference to tasks. In everyday understanding, however, we merge these two concepts. While we make a distinction between tacit and explicit intelligence, it is important to note that this distinction does not correspond to the distinction between conscious and unconscious. In fact, the precise role of consciousness in intelligence is far from clear. We tend to think of intelligence as the conscious exercise of certain faculties, but there is mounting evidence that consciousness does not play so central a role as we like to think. A notorious example is the phenomenon of "blindsight." Persons with this affliction have the subjective experience of blindness. They insist that they cannot see anything and that their visual field is simply a void. They have no visual qualia. Despite the subjective blindness, their eyes are capable of functioning to some extent and they are capable of pointing to sources of light. If you ask such a person how he is able to guess correctly, he'll tell you that he doesn't know, that he "felt" it, or that it was just a lucky guess. Paradoxical as it sounds, the best way to describe this phenomenon is to say that the person "sees" but does not have any visual experiences. His vision occurs without the participation of visual consciousness or subjectivity.

To take another example, it is also known that fairly elaborate problem solving takes place without the participation of consciousness. A computer programmer might go to sleep with a complicated programming problem on his mind and wake up the next morning fully aware of the solution. We might say that his unconscious mind solved the problem, or alternatively that he solved the problem while unconscious. We know that unconscious problem solving is by no means unusual and that some people have come to count on it. In fact, the very notion of conscious problem solving is not as clear as it once seemed to be. When individuals are given complex problems to solve and asked to say aloud what steps they go through in solving them, the surprising finding is that the steps of which they are conscious, which they claim are the steps that lead them to the solution, often are of only marginal relevance to the solution of the problem. The individual thinks that he is consciously solving a problem, but may in fact only be paying attention to marginal details while the actual problem solving is going on unconsciously.

In short, it is becoming increasingly difficult to say just what consciousness is *for*. Even language use can occur without consciousness, as in the case of talking in one's sleep. It is fairly easy to see why evolution has endowed humans with intelligence. Intelligence, after all, is precisely our ability to cope with the world. To the extent that we are better able to cope, our chances of survival are increased, and intelligence is therefore favored by natural selection. It is not so easy to see why we, or any other creatures, are endowed with consciousness. It becomes even less easy the more we learn about the possibility of intelligence without the involvement of consciousness. If we could be just as intelligent without being conscious, then why has nature gone to the trouble of endowing us with consciousness? If we concede the point that even creatures far less intelligent than us are nevertheless not less conscious than us, the link between intelligence and consciousness is correspondingly weakened.

Caution is important here, however. The fact of the matter is that we just don't know whether consciousness is necessary for the full range of human intelligence. We don't know if consciousness is necessary for the full range of animal intelligence. It is tempting to suppose that it must be necessary or else we wouldn't have evolved to have it, but we don't know that either. In the absence of a detailed theory of intelligence and consciousness, all we can do is conjecture. But these caveats have considerable significance for the philosophy of artificial intelligence. Again, we are simply not in a position to say that a given programmed digital program is or is not intelligent unless we can say with some confidence what the role of consciousness and intelligence is and what it is for a programmed computer to be conscious. Without some theoretically solid answers to these questions, the attribution of intelligence to programmed digital computers remains conjectural.

Because human beings who use ordinary human language aim at a kind of clarity that is quite different from what philosophers want, the terms that we most often use to refer to mental states and processes are vague with respect to consciousness. Beliefs, for example, are mental states, but we are not necessarily conscious of all of our beliefs. Still, we might insist that we *could* be conscious of any of our beliefs. We think of perception as a paradigmatically conscious process until we think about blindsight. My idea is that while consciousness may be intimately associated with those states that we call mental states, it is not just another one of those mental states. Consciousness is not a mental state in the way that believing, fearing, hoping, planning, and problem solving may be thought of as mental states. The possibility of being associated with consciousness may be what makes those mental states mental, but consciousness itself remains distinguishable from them.

Chapter 6

Connections

In the chapter about the general nature of computing machines and formal systems, I presented a fairly low-level description of computing. That is, I described the process as involving the automated manipulation of digital tokens according to rules. You may recall that I avoided calling these tokens "symbols," even though that is just how one might think about them on an intuitive level.

My reason for avoiding the term "symbol" at that point was to avoid prejudicing the discussion in favor of a certain AI programming strategy, sometimes referred to as "symbolic processing." Although this strategy has dominated the AI field for some time, a recent rival is the strategy called "connectionism."[1] In this chapter, I hope to provide a clear explanation of how connectionism does and does not differ from symbolic processing and what difference it might make to the various philosophical issues in the philosophy of AI.

Symbolic Processing

Consider again a statement that I made in an earlier chapter: "To call a token a symbol is already to indicate that it bears some meaning or is subject to an interpretation." Now recall that in a digital (elec-

---

1. It is misleading to say that connectionism is "recent," since it has been around about as long as symbolic processing. What is recent is the enthusiasm for it in the AI mainstream.

tronic) computer, the tokens are sequences of digits in memory locations.[2] As the computer executes its program, it manipulates these tokens.

The computer program, you will recall, consists of instructions such as "total_score:=alice+bill+carol." The words here were referred to as "identifiers." When the computer executes this instruction, it refers to a place in memory that the programming language allows you, the programmer, to refer to as "total_score." The programming language is designed in this way to make it easier for you to keep track of what the program is doing. The computer also refers to three other memory locations, performs the operation of addition on the tokens (we would call them "values") stored there, and puts the sum in the location called "total_score." So the identifiers are words that the programming language allows the programmer to use as names with which to refer to the contents of memory at various locations.

It should be obvious that the programmer has used the words "total_score," "alice," "bill," and "carol" because these are meaningful in the context of the task at hand. She wants the program to compute the total score on some test taken by Alice, Bill, and Carol. So, while those words, as they occur in the high-level programming language Pascal, refer to memory contents, those memory contents—the physical tokens that are manipulated—refer to the test scores of some people and the sum of those scores. If we think of the simple task for which the program was written as a world, then the tokens refer to objects in that task-world.

It is also obvious that what the tokens refer to depends upon what program the computer is executing. In this case, a given set of memory locations stores a string that refers to Alice's test score; another program might use the very same locations to refer to Alice's height, or the perihelion of Venus, or anything at all. Clearly, the reference in the task-world depends upon the task, which depends upon the intentions and understanding of the programmer and users of the program.[3]

---

2. Well, physically they are configurations of discrete voltage states in silicon locations; what we are calling "digits" are just the names that we give to those configurations.

These intentions establish a *mapping* between the tokens and the objects in the task-world.

Now consider a more complex task, such as chess playing. Think about it as a programmer might. You'll need an array of memory locations to refer to the squares of a chessboard, and you'll need a coding system to refer to the pieces on those squares. You will also need to keep track of such things as whether the king is in check, whether a piece is threatened, whose move it is, and so forth. In fact, as a programmer your job is to identify all of the aspects of the task that need to be referred to in the program. We may think of this as defining the task-world. Then you need to figure out the best structures[4] for referring to them and the algorithms for manipulating them.

I have introduced the concept of a "task-world" casually in order to make certain points, but there is a great deal built into this concept. If we suppose that the computer is to be programmed to perform some actual task in the real world, such as playing chess, the task-world will comprise all of the objects of the real world that are relevant to that task, and the relevant properties of those objects. It consists of everything that needs to be kept track of to get the job done. The chessboard is clearly a relevant object, but the table on which it rests is not. The relevant "states" of the squares of the chessboard will have to do with which pieces are resting on those squares, not with the particular colors of the squares on the board.

The task-world is an abstraction. Its contents are determined by "relevance," and it is the programmer's job to decide what is relevant. She will want identifiers or data structures of some sort to refer to all and only the objects in the task-world. She won't bother having an identifier for the table on which the game is played, or to represent

---

3. After all, I might decide to use this very same program to compute some other average of three numbers, in which case the reference of the tokens would have nothing at all to do with Alice, Bill, and Carol.

4. A "data structure" is a technical concept that need not concern us too much here. Suffice it to say that the programming languages allow memory locations to be grouped and referred to by identifiers in a number of ways that make it easier for the programmer to establish the mapping between the tokens and the objects in the task-world.

whether the pieces are made of wood or plastic. In the case of chess, it is fairly obvious what belongs in the task-world and what does not.

The essence of the symbolic-processing approach to AI, then, is to posit a task-world and to write a program such that the memory-tokens of the computer can refer directly to the objects in the task-world. The states of the computer will have as their "meaning" the states of the task-world. Furthermore, the rules according to which tokens are manipulated will correspond to the rules governing the behavior of the objects in the task-world. These rules describe the actual behavior of the real-world objects in which the programmer is interested. The program, considered as data structure and an algorithm for manipulating it, is an explicit representation of those objects.

It is important to consider the implications of symbolic processing not only for such restricted tasks as chess playing but for the more ambitious task of passing the Turing Test. What would be in the task-world? Words, clearly, would be some of the objects. Just as clearly, the task-world would have to have much more than words; it would need to include, somehow, meanings or ideas, and rules for manipulating them. In short, if the task is to give a computer a mind, then according to the symbolic-processing strategy the memory-tokens will have to refer to mental objects of some sort: ideas, concepts, meanings, or whatever. The programmed computer will manipulate these tokens according to much the same rules with which the objects are manipulated in the mind itself. The algorithm specified in the program will be just like the "rules" of thinking. If, as some have argued, rationality is essential to human thought, then the program will need to include a representation of some model of rationality. We have already seen that it is by no means a simple matter to develop such a model, and that it goes far beyond the possibilities of formal logic.

The symbolic-processing approach to AI, then, is more than just a programming strategy; it is a *theory* about the way the mind works. Adding the modest materialistic assumption that the way the mind works depends upon the way the brain works, it is a theory according to which the brain itself has token-states that refer to objects and states of the world, and manipulates these tokens according to rules that may be represented by algorithms. The symbolic-processing strategy of AI is based on the assumption that it is the right approach because it is the approach used by the brain itself. Quoting Hubert and Stuart Dreyfus,

> Computers are general symbol manipulators, so they can simulate any process which can be described exactly. When digital computers were actually constructed they were first used for scientific calculation. But, as noted, by the end of the 1950s researchers like Allen Newell and Herbert Simon began to take seriously the idea that computers were general symbol manipulators. They saw that one could use symbols to represent elementary facts about the world and use rules to represent relationships between them. Computers could then follow such rules or programs to deduce how those facts affect each other and what happens when the facts change. In this way computers came to be used to simulate logical thinking.[5]

The simulation of logical thinking is central to the development of symbolic-processing AI, which is why I was at some pains in an earlier chapter to give an introductory account of logic as a formal system. Although there are probably few, if any, AI workers who would explicitly claim that logical inference is the "mark of the mental," there does seem to be a tacit assumption in symbolic AI that *rule following* is the mark of the mental. Moreover, rule following is a logical process.

It is safe to say that the symbolic-processing strategy has dominated the field of AI until relatively recently, and even now it is by no means defunct. In fact, for the reader who is not already familiar with other strategies, it may be difficult even to conceive of alternatives. As I have described the chess program above, for example, the symbolic-processing approach seems inevitable. Chess has objects and rules for manipulating them. It makes perfect sense to use the flexibility of a programmable computer to represent the objects in memory and to encode as an algorithm the manipulation rules. How else could it be done?

Before moving to a discussion of connectionism, then, it will be worthwhile to consider some of the difficulties inherent in the symbolic-processing approach to AI. Keep in mind that there is no consensus

---

5.   Dreyfus and Dreyfus, *Mind over Machine*, p. 53.

within the AI research community about whether these difficulties are insurmountable or, even if not insurmountable, whether it is a good idea to pursue the symbolic-processing approach to surmounting them.

Difficulties

We may turn our attention once again to the Turing Test, and take the passing of the Turing Test to be the task at hand. As I have already mentioned, the task-world will need to be very complex indeed. It will have to include not only a complete formal description of a natural language—if that is even possible—but it will also have to include some sort of representation of each belief about the world, various affective tags on these beliefs, and more. In an earlier chapter, we noted that Hubert Dreyfus has argued that linguistic competence cannot be considered apart from many or all of the other faculties that language-users have. His argument was aimed precisely at the symbolic-processing approach to AI. What he was really criticizing is the attempt to base AI on a supposedly complete formal description of the mind.

The point that should now be apparent is that what I have been calling a task-world is just a formal theory of the domain of interest. To maintain that the definition of a task-world can be completed is to maintain that a formal theory can be devised. In the case of certain sorts of processes, such as chess playing,[6] this is a correct assumption. The game of chess is, after all, an artifact of the human mind, an invented formal system. Even though the game of chess is much older than the modern theory of formal systems, it embodies such theory very clearly.

The conclusion clearly is that symbolic AI is most promising when applied to problems where a task-world can be clearly (if not necessarily simply) defined. Considering the Turing Test as a problem, it is a matter of controversy whether this is likely or even possible. To pass the Turing Test one must know more than just rules for "processing" sentences of a natural language, even though one must clearly know *some* rules of this

---

6.   Even here, a caveat is necessary. Although the rules to the game of chess can be specified in a formal theory, it does not follow that every way of playing a legal game can be so specified.

sort. The Turing Test doesn't attempt to test merely whether a system can process sentences; it's supposed to determine whether the system can *talk*, or make sense, or understand, or whatever. To generate "appropriate" responses, the system must be able to express a plausible set of beliefs about the world. The main point of the Dreyfus "holism" argument is that human understanding of natural language and understanding of the things that humans talk about are interpenetrating. One cannot be separated from the other. To attempt to derive a finished set of rules for just talking, one must make arbitrary assumptions. Dreyfus and Dreyfus write:

> The sort of rules human beings are able to articulate always contain *ceteris paribus* conditions. Moreover, there is not just one exception to each rule but several, and all the rules for dealing with the exceptions are also *ceteris paribus* rules. So we get not only a regress of rules for applying rules but an exponential explosion of them; the number of rules required multiplies at an ever increasing rate.[7]

One reply that is often offered to the Holism argument is that the problem cannot be as intractable as it seems because we human beings are obviously embodiments of its solution. Somehow, we manage to implement and follow the set of rules that enables us to use and understand natural language. There must therefore be a way to encode those rules into the memory of a digital computer.

The trouble is, we don't know if we achieve our linguistic competence by following rules at all. To understand this, we need to think more carefully about what it means for a system to follow a rule.

Following Rules

The word "rule" is troublesome because it has a descriptive sense according to which *every* deterministic process can be described as "following a rule." Water flows downhill. The rate at which it flows, and other aspects of its flow are described and predicted (within limits) by

---

7. Dreyfus and Dreyfus, *Mind over Machine*, p. 80.

the equations of fluid dynamics. In a sense, it "follows the rules" of fluid dynamics, just as the planets in their orbits follow the rules of Newtonian mechanics.

In the same sense, the electronic circuit gates of a digital computer follow the rules of semiconductor physics and the neurons in the brain follow other bioelectrical rules. But this is not the sense of rule following that is at stake in symbolic processing. There, the rules are at a higher level of description. They exist as meanings in the program that the programmer creates. For example, the chess programmer might encode a rule that stipulates that the program should never enter into a material exchange that involves the loss of a queen, even if the opponent's material loss is greater.[8] So the programmed computer will avoid queen sacrifices, even when they might result in relative material gain for the computer. It will follow this rule even though at a strictly physical level of description all it *ever* does is follow the rules of semiconductor physics. You could not tell, by a purely physical inspection of the computer as it passes from one state to another, that it was following the queen rule at all.

But here's another thing. It could turn out that, even if the queen rule were not programmed into it, the computer would avoid queen sacrifices just as if it were. That is, behavior that "follows" the queen rule could be *emergent* behavior that results from the computer simultaneously following a number of other rules that have been explicitly programmed in. Furthermore, there would be no way, just by looking at the way the computer plays, to decide whether it is acting on a coded rule or an emergent rule.

The distinction between coded and emergent rules is relevant and important as long as we think about the computer as a system that must be programmed to get a task done. Thinking through the possible emergent rules is a large and difficult part of debugging a program, since emergent rules can hinder as well as enhance performance. When we think about the machine apart from its programmer, simply doing whatever it does, the distinction is less clear. Again, there would be no way to tell, by looking at its behavior or directly inspecting its memory

---

8. Needless to say, this would not be a terrific rule to encode, but at least it's clear.

locations, whether a given rule that it is "following" in its behavior is coded or emergent.

Now consider this: Maybe it would be possible to program a computer to play chess by having *all* of its chess-playing behavior be the result of emergent rules. How could this be? Perhaps it could be done by having all of the explicitly coded rules be at the subsymbolic level. This rather mysterious proposition brings us finally to the other main strategy for creating AI: connectionism.

Connectionism

The best way to understand connectionism is to approach it from the standpoint of hardware. Conventional computers do their work by *sequential processing*. That is, they have a single CPU that performs one computation at a time, at the rate of millions per second. No two computations are performed simultaneously.[9] This is not the only way to do things. Another approach would be to have many CPUs working simultaneously, sharing the results of computations when necessary. This is called *parallel processing*.

A major advantage of parallel processing is speed. Many hands make light work and many processors make fast work, for the same reason. A difficulty from a purely technical standpoint is the complexity of managing the flow of information. The separate processors must share the right information at the right time or the result will be chaos.

The idea behind the connectionist approach to AI is this: Instead of trying to code an explicit set of rules and symbols of the task-world, let such rulelike activity emerge from the interaction of a network of relatively simple processors.

Imagine a grid of tiny computers programmed (or hardwired) only to do addition and to execute a single conditional instruction: If the sum is greater than n, then send the number 1 to the next processor; otherwise send zero. As inputs, each processor receives numbers from adjoining

---

9.   Actually, this is an oversimplification. Even relatively unsophisticated home computers may have separate processors for managing sound and video tasks, but what we may think of as the "main" computing is done sequentially in a single CPU.

processors. Suppose each processor receives an input from ten others, either a 1 or a 0. It adds them up and compares them to some number n. Let's say that n is 5. The result would be that if a given processor gets a 1 from six or more of its input processors, it will send a 1 as output to some other processor; otherwise it will send a 0. Whatever it sends will be handled in the same way by that processor, and so on through the network. The connections between the processors may be as complex as you like.

Up to this point, the connection machine sounds like a busy but useless device for doing lots of trivial arithmetic problems, but nothing more. Now consider a few more complications. Suppose first of all that some of the processors in the network get their input not from other processors but from some other sort of input device. Perhaps there is a bank of processors, each of which receives a 1 or a 0 from a pixel of a photographed image, a digital picture. Suppose also that the value of n, the "connection strength variable," can vary in each processor as the traffic flow at that processor varies. If this activity were handled properly, the entire network might be able to learn to recognize pictures. The "state" of such a machine would be the interaction between its inputs and the connection strengths among its component processors. It could "remember" an image without there being any explicitly coded representation of the image or an explicitly coded set of rules for recognizing things. The memory would be distributed throughout the network as the values of n are modified, as opposed to having an explicit data structure such as an array in which the values are stored.

If the remembered image is an image of, say, Voltaire, there would be no data structure that explicitly refers to his nose, or chin, or even a photographic pixel. Instead, we say that the actual computing is at the "subsymbolic" level. That is, all the adding and comparing of numbers that is going on in the network at any given moment doesn't "stand for" anything; it's only the activity needed to enable the network to function. The network learns and remembers as the connections between the processors are adjusted. Quoting again from Dreyfus and Dreyfus:

When used to realize a distributed associative memory, computers are no longer functioning as symbol-manipulating systems in which the symbols represent features of the world and computations express relationships among the features as in conventional AI. Instead, the computer simulates a holistic system.[10]

I have suggested the possibility of connecting a connection machine to some sort of visual input system because connectionist models of vision have a long history in AI and psychology. The core problem is to get the system to identify three-dimensional objects from the two-dimensional array of inputs presented to it. Early attempts to make computers "see" were not connectionist, but rather involved the symbolic coding of property lists and a formal system for making inferences. That is, the programmer would encode some sort of algorithm for recognizing a pattern as an edge or a surface, and then would apply a set of rules for making an identification. Later efforts refined this approach. The connectionist approach still involves "feature detection," but the features are not detected by means of a symbolically coded algorithm. The "property lists" are distributed throughout the system.

Note that a problem for both approaches is the fact that seeing involves more than interpreting a two-dimensional input array: It makes extensive use of *knowledge* of the objects that are seen. In the case of optical illusions, this knowledge may lead us to "see" things that aren't there.

What I have given here is only the most simplistic description of a connectionist architecture, glossing over the very difficult technical details. The purpose is to get the reader to understand how a connection machine might work, in general terms. To those with some understanding of the physiology of the brain, the description of a connection machine may seem rather familiar. The neurons in the brain are believed to be networked in a similar way, generating action potentials along an axon depending upon the sum of inputs from a large number of dendrites (in some cases, thousands of them). In the case

---

10. Dreyfus and Dreyfus, *Mind over Machine*, p. 91.

of neurons, the inputs and outputs may be excitatory or inhibitory. It is as if we allowed positive or negative 1's to be used in our computer model.

The similarity between the connection machine as I have described it and the brain is certainly no accident. The brain is the inspiration for the connection machine, and, in fact, the type of connectionist architecture that I have described in general terms is called a *neural network*. There are other possible connectionist architectures, but neural networks have the strongest intuitive pull. After all, if the brain itself can accomplish real intelligence, true cognition, by means of the activity of a vast network of neurons, why shouldn't a computer-based neural network system accomplish the same thing?

Within the AI research community, there are many disputes about what sorts of tasks neural networks and other connectionist architectures can reasonably be expected to perform. Brain researchers argue about the details of how actual neural processing might work. Psychologists argue about the ways in which various cognitive tasks might be accomplished. The attempt to develop models of the mind and brain that are based upon possible architectures and programming of computing systems is called *computational psychology*, and connectionism is one of its leading research paradigms. But variations on the symbolic-processing approach have by no means been abandoned. It is one thing to say that the brain is a network of neurons and quite another to call it a neural network in the computational sense that the term has come to have. Computer scientists who design connection machines may have objectives that are quite different from those of the computational psychologists who devise connectionist models of cognition. In both groups, there is a wide spectrum of opinion about how to proceed. These disputes are for the most part technical and, although they have important consequences for methodology in these fields, tend to obscure somewhat the central philosophical issues involved. This is, after all, a book about the *philosophy* of artificial intelligence, so it is important that we should turn to a consideration of the impact, if any, of connectionism on the philosophical issues surrounding artificial intelligence.

Philosophical Implications

There are several things to be noted about the connectionist approach to AI. First, a true connection machine must be realized in a parallel-processing architecture. This is an architecture whose efficiency in certain kinds of tasks offers a tentative answer to the question, raised in the previous chapter, of how the relatively slow neural network of the brain is able to accomplish many tasks, such as recognition, almost instantaneously. Second, any parallel-processing connection machine can be *simulated* on a sequential machine. Third, a true connection machine is not within the critical scope of Searle's Chinese Room argument.

Concerning the first point, the case for massively parallel processing in the brain must not be underestimated. Even though we know very little about the processing-level details of the brain's functioning, we should give serious consideration to any hypothesis that suggests an answer to the puzzle of how the brain does certain things as quickly as it does. However, there is still much to be learned here. At the present time, the most that one can say is that there are a few working connectionist toy programs (i.e., programs that succeed with simplified tasks in artificially restricted domains), and the brain may well function along similar lines.

The second point, that any connection machine can be simulated on a sequential machine, needs careful examination. What is it for one kind of computer to simulate another kind of computer?

To answer this, remember that the connection machine comprises a large number of simple processors sharing the results of their computations. At any given moment each of these little processors is in a particular state, and that state must be precisely determinable, depending upon its previous state and the states of the processors to which it is linked. Now consider this possibility: Instead of actually building such a machine, with all of its complex hardware requirements, we'll take a suitably large sequential computer—that's with only one processor, remember—and we'll write a program to simulate the connection machine. In that program, we will define a large data structure, elements of which will "behave" as the small processors of the connection machine behave. The program will assign to these elements just the "states" that those processors would be in. Thus, the input/output behavior of the sequential simulation will be just what that of the connection machine would have been.

One way to visualize this rather difficult concept is to think of the connection machine as an army of bookkeepers who receive phone calls from each other, do some calculations on their adding machines, and telephone other bookkeepers with the results. For the simulation, imagine that each bookkeeper has been replaced with a cardboard simulacrum. There is, however, a *super*-bookkeeper who zips from one bookkeeper's desk to another, does the calculations for her, makes the phone calls, and zooms on (fast enough to answer those phone calls, when necessary). The super-bookkeeper will get the work done and, if he is fast enough, he'll get it done as quickly as the army of bookkeepers would have.

This is how a single processor can simulate a network of processors. Furthermore, it is by means of simulations that most actual research into connection machines is done. It is prohibitively expensive, in terms of materials and time, to be assembling and dismantling connection machines from scratch for each new research hypothesis when a simulation can test the hypothesis just as decisively. The only difference is one of speed. Unless it is very fast indeed, the sequential simulation is likely to be slower than the connection machine.

What we can say about the connection machine and its sequential simulation is that, speed considerations aside, they are functionally equivalent. They do the same work, input for input and output for output. Recall that one of the ways of stating the point of the Turing Test is that systems that are functionally equivalent are mentally equivalent. Before accepting or rejecting that claim, though, consider the next point raised at the beginning of this section.

I stated that a connection machine that passes the Turing Test would not be susceptible to Searle's Chinese Room objection. Why not? Because the human being in the Chinese Room—the one looking up things in the huge manual—is supposed to be the embodiment of the single CPU of the sequential computer. In a connection machine, however, there is no *single* CPU; there is a multitude of them. You would need an army of humans, rather like the army of bookkeepers mentioned above. Each one would have only a very small manual of instructions, perhaps only a single instruction. Whatever the intuitive appeal of that scenario might be, it is clear that it is not the same as Searle's own. There can be no man in the Chinese Room who is just "doing what the computer does," since a connection machine is really not a single computer. The philosopher Dale Jacquette makes the point in the following way:

> The information-processing system micro-functionally isomorphic to a native Chinese speaker might not have a single locus of control, and the execution of its input-to-output transformation program might be distributed throughout rather than concentrated somewhere within its procedural network.[11]

Note that "micro-functional isomorphism" means a strong similarity between this information-processing system (Jacquette does not use the word "computer" here) and the brain of a human native Chinese speaker, at the level of actual neural-signaling architecture, presumably. So, if a connection machine of this (or any) sort were to pass the Turing Test, Searle's Chinese Room argument could not possibly show that the machine does not have genuine mental states. Needless to say, the failure of Searle's argument does not entail that the connection machine *have* genuine mental states, either.

At this point, we reach an interesting riddle: Searle's Chinese Room argument *does* apply to any sequential simulation of a Turing Test–passing connection machine, since it presumably applies to any sequential machine at all. The simulation is, by definition, functionally equivalent to the connection machine being simulated. In effect, we now have three classes of machine under consideration, each of which might in principle pass the Turing Test:

---

11. Dale Jacquette, "Adventures in the Chinese Room," *Philosophy and Phenomenological Research*, 49, no. 4 (June 1989), 608-9.

1. A sequential computer programmed according to the symbolic processing approach.

2. A connection machine.

3. A sequential computer programmed symbolically to simulate a Turing Test-passing connection machine.

The three machines are functionally equivalent, but what is going on inside the black box is very different. The question is: Do these differences make what philosophers would call an *ontological* difference? Does one enjoy a real mental life while the other two are mere mechanical impostors? Let's review the arguments that can be brought to bear.

The first machine, a symbolically programmed sequential machine, is the sort of attempt at artificial intelligence that Dreyfus especially targeted. Remember, though, that Dreyfus's attack deals primarily with the *feasibility* of this approach to AI. He thinks it extremely unlikely that any such machine will ever pass the Turing Test. Here we are asking: If such a machine *did* pass the Turing Test, what then? Dreyfus's argument does not explicitly address that hypothesis, but Searle's does.

Searle's argument is that no programmed computer could possess mental states solely in virtue of being programmed in a certain way. It is, you recall, the "causal powers" of the brain that produce the mental phenomena, as apart from its formal or computational properties. Thus, this rules out the third machine, the connection-machine simulation, as well.

The second machine, however, can be plausibly said to be different from the other two at the level of its "causal powers." At least this much can be said: The connection machine does not achieve its (hypothesized) linguistic competence solely by executing a program. Indeed, it is not "programmed" at all in the standard sense of the term. Its component processors are programmed, but in a sense that is no more relevant to language and semantics than the "programming" of a biological neuron. It does what it does by means of continuous modifications of the "strength" of connections between processors, not by manipulating memory values that represent objects in a task-world. In a sense, the connection machine is not a computer at all; it is a system that happens to be *made of* computers.

Searle argues that the brain does not achieve understanding and most other Intentional mental phenomena simply through its computational powers. He does not argue that neurons—or even modules of neurons—do not do what they do in virtue of their computational powers. It is not farfetched to conceive of an individual neuron or a functionally connected group of neurons as a computer. As we have seen, it makes perfect sense to describe them as computers that add inputs and execute a conditional instruction. That the brain is made of such computers does not entail that it is one.

You will recall that Searle's claim is not that no artificial system can have mental states but that any system that does so must duplicate the causal powers of the brain. It is time, then, to undertake a more careful examination of what these causal powers might be.

Causal Powers

Searle's view, repeatedly stated, is that computers can only simulate certain properties of brains—its formal or computational properties— because computers are only capable of formal, or syntactic, operations. The semantic side of things, which comprises the content, meaning, or reference of mental states, must come from some other properties. These are the causal properties, the properties by means of which certain brain processes cause certain mental processes.

We have already taken note of the obvious fact that the computational processes that take place in a computer or a brain or anywhere else are causal processes. We must understand Searle to be claiming that the causal powers involved in computation either are not the right ones or are not sufficient (though they could be necessary) to produce mental processes. We may ask how Searle knows that they are not sufficient, and he will drag out the Chinese Room again. The Chinese Room gets the computational powers and nothing else, and it doesn't produce a system that understands Chinese, so something else must be involved in producing understanding. Searle takes this to be fundamental, as is shown in the following remarks:

> It is important to emphasize again that we are not talking about a particular stage of computer technology. The argument has nothing to do with the forthcoming, amazing advances in computer science. It has nothing to do with the distinction between serial and parallel processes, or with the size of programs, or the speed of computer operations, or with computers that can interact causally with their environment, or even with the invention of robots.[12]

Can this be right? Searle claims that his argument has nothing to do with the distinction between serial (sequential) and parallel processes, but we have already seen that this is wrong. A true parallel-processing connection machine is not subject to his argument, although a sequential simulation of it is. Searle himself, however, is at pains to assert, "[N]o simulation by itself ever constitutes duplication."[13] A simulated connection machine is not a connection machine. I have said that "in a sense" the connection machine is not a computer at all, although it is made of computers. I said this because the causal principles of its global operation are so very different from the paradigm computers, which are sequential machines.

Searle writes,

> If it really is a computer, its operations have to be defined syntactically, whereas consciousness, thoughts, feelings, emotions, and all the rest of it involve more than a syntax. Those features, by definition, the computer is unable to *duplicate* however powerful may be its ability to *simulate*.[14]

Are the operations of a connection machine "defined syntactically"? It is hard to know what to make of this. The fact that the operation of a connection machine can be simulated on a sequential machine entails that its behavior can be *described* syntactically by the right

---

12.   Searle, *Minds, Brains and Science*, p. 36.
13.   Ibid., p. 37.
14.   Ibid.

computer program. But so can any deterministic process. Searle himself says,

> From a mathematical point of view, anything whatever can be described *as if* it were a digital computer. And that's because it can be described as instantiating or implementing a computer program.[15]

Sure. But the behavior of the sort of connection machine we are considering is not following the rules or instructions of a program; it is "following" *emergent* rules. It seems to me that the ability to do so is precisely the sort of thing that the causal powers of the brain must be about. In a real sense, the operation of the connection machine involves "more than a syntax." It involves connectivity, which is defined architecturally, not syntactically.

Searle's position has evolved somewhat since he wrote *Minds, Brains and Programs* in 1980. More recently, he has argued that the very notion of describing a system by its syntax engenders certain difficulties. I touched on this in Chapter 3, but Searle's view of these difficulties is worth considering again in the present context. Noting that a given syntactical or formal structure can be realized in any number of different physical systems, he writes,

> If computation is defined in terms of the assignment of syntax then everything would be a digital computer, because any object whatever could have syntactical ascriptions made to it. You could describe anything in terms of 0's and 1's. Worse yet, syntax is not intrinsic to physics. The ascription of syntactical properties is always relative to an agent or observer who treats certain physical phenomena as syntactical.[16]

But even though there may be some sense in which anything at all is a digital computer, there is also an empirical sense in which digital computers and connection machines are different sorts of things. A connection machine is not just a digital computer "under a different

---

15.   Ibid., p. 36.
16.   Searle, "Is the Brain a Digital Computer?" p. 26.

description." At least, there is nothing to be gained by so characterizing it. These systems have different architectures, which means that their parts interact with each other and with the world in fundamentally different ways. It makes sense to call this a difference in causal powers.

Furthermore, such mental phenomena as understanding *must* have something to do with a system's ability to interact causally with the world. An important part of your understanding of the word "green" is your having had certain visual experiences that were caused by your eyes interacting with light. If you were congenitally blind, you could not have this understanding, no matter how glib you might be in your use of the word "green" and its cognates. The point should be obvious: To understand a color word is not simply to be able to use it intelligibly in sentences. It is to be able to do so because one has had certain experiences, namely visual experience of that color. The same point can be made for all terms that include qualia as essential to their meaning. Being able to interact with the world, indeed, has something to do with understanding.

If you think about your own experience of using language, you will notice that it involves the manipulation of symbols in ways that are determined (in part) by your nonlinguistic experiences. In order to "experience" a symbol—a word or an utterance—*as* a symbol and not a mere token, there must be some mapping between your linguistic or semiotic experiences[17] and your other, nonlinguistic experiences. Your understanding of the symbols consists in part of your ability to create, maintain, and update this mapping, to modify it in the light of further experiences. The digital computer in a metal box, accepting input strings and generating output strings, has no nonlinguistic "experiences" to map, because its only interaction with the world is its exchange of these strings. It's clear enough, even without invoking the Chinese Room argument, that such an entity is not capable of understanding, but it should also be clear that its interactions with the world do make a difference, contrary to what Searle maintains above.

We should not lose sight of the distinction that was carefully made

---

17.   The word "semiotic" refers to all symbols, not just linguistic ones.

in an earlier chapter between consciousness and the rest of the range of mental phenomena. While we may be able to assimilate understanding and other mental processes into a connectionist model, consciousness remains as mysterious as ever. It is no more clear how a network of processors could be conscious than it is clear how a brain can be conscious. If, as I have maintained, it is consciousness that makes certain processes experiences, then we must be careful of referring to any processes going on in any artifact, be they linguistic processes or not, as experiences. We simply do not know what the criteria are for describing a process as an experience.

Coming back to the case of understanding, it may be useful to cleave the concept into a number of tributary concepts. First, there is the aspect of understanding that *is* detected by the Turing Test, the ability to accept certain linguistic tokens and respond with appropriate replies. Since this is the ability to function like a competent natural-language user, we may call this "F-understanding." Since it is possible that F-understanding can be achieved in more than one way—to wit, in a sequential or a connection machine—we may say that the ability to do so in a way that "duplicates the causal powers of the brain," to use Searle's phrase, is "C-understanding." Next, there is the aspect of understanding that is the result of interactive mapping of linguistic objects onto nonlinguistic inputs, which helps to sustain the intentionality of the states. We may call this "I-understanding." Finally, there is the experienced or subjective part of understanding, the part that makes it like something to understand, in Nagel's words. This subjective part we may call "S-understanding."

I believe that what we actually mean by "understanding" comprises all of these. But concepts are not static entities; they are altered by new discoveries, old insights, arguments, and research programs. Much of the philosophical dispute in the philosophy of AI can be seen as a struggle over which of these aspects of the concept of understanding is somehow essential or central.[18]

---

18. And I hope it is clear that these observations can apply equally well to many other mental concepts.

The functionalist, for example, maintains that F-understanding is sufficient for understanding, with no prefixes. Searle may be understood as insisting that F-understanding be achieved by means of C-understanding. Others, myself included, would make the requirements even tighter, insisting that I-understanding be realized. Finally, it is certainly tempting to insist on S-understanding, even though it is far from clear how to give content to this insistence.

With these distinctions in hand, we can expose an interesting quirk of Searle's Chinese Room argument. Although Searle's position is that F-understanding is insufficient for understanding because it does not guarantee C-understanding, the actual scenario shows that it is S-understanding that is lacking! The person in the Chinese Room does not have the *experience* of understanding, so the system doesn't understand. That is the force of the argument, since the reader is supposed to place herself by means of imagination in the Chinese Room to "verify" that she would not understand any Chinese. This exercise would have no point unless it were presupposed that she would *know* whether or not she understands Chinese, that she would recognize that experience if she had it. This is the actual logical content of the argument, as opposed to what Searle alleges is its content.

In this chapter, I have tried to explain a number of rather complex distinctions involving sequential processing, connection machines, coded and emergent rules, and so on. In addition, I have tried to establish the connections between these concepts and many others discussed in earlier chapters. The reader should have at least a general sense of the conceptual territory and why it is so embattled at the present time. It is not just about computers; it is about the very concepts that we have used to think about ourselves, such as understanding, thinking, believing, and knowing. It is much more about who we are than about what computers can do. The next chapter, then, moves away from this conceptual terrain and attempts a cursory exploration of how the development of artificial intelligence may affect us as beings with a social and moral nature.

Chapter 7

Machines and Selves

So far, our attention has been engaged in trying to understand the nature of computing machines and the philosophical puzzles central to that nature. Although I cannot pretend to have solved those puzzles, I believe it is important to pass on to a consideration of how artificial intelligence has influenced thinking about other matters. It was my contention in Chapter 1 that this influence has already been profound and is by no means finished. One of the reasons for my brief review of formal logic (in addition to providing what I believe is a necessary background to the philosophical study of artificial intelligence) was to show how this classical domain of study has blossomed in the twentieth century, hand-in-hand with the development of the theory of computing machines.

There are two interrelated topics that I shall proceed to examine in the light of the appearance of artificial intelligence on the intellectual scene. First, there is the problem of personal identity. Briefly, this is how philosophers refer to the problem of saying precisely just what it is for a person to be the *same* person over time. As trivial and obvious as this question may seem to the uninitiated, it quickly leads into some very deep water.

Second, there is the conception of personhood *by* persons, and the social and moral implications of changes in that conception. There is no question that new technologies affect the way we see and understand ourselves. It is no accident that the industrial revolution was accompanied by a more mechanical conception of the person, and it is inevitable that what is coming to be called the "information age" should have equally profound effects. I will attempt to summarize what a few people are saying about this.

Personal Identity

You are born, live for a time, and die. You may be able to remember some experiences from early childhood; some claim to remember their own births. It is natural enough to view life as a stream of experiences, as we did in Chapter 2. What we did not do at that time, however, was to ask just what it means to say that those experiences are the experiences of a single enduring person.

It is possible, of course, to reject the idea that one is a single, enduring, individual person who exists at each moment of a span of time called a life. One of the things we shall try to do here is explore whether artificial intelligence has strengthened or weakened the basis of such a rejection. It remains true, nevertheless, that the notion of persons enduring over time is widely accepted, both in common speech and in philosophical discourse. No one denies that persons undergo many and constant changes, some of which may be so radical as to count as upheavals, or breakdowns, or transformations. We even on occasion use the language of discontinuity and say that someone is "not the same person," though it is doubtful that we mean this in the most literal sense. But this is precisely the sense that is at stake here.

Like all philosophical questions, the question of personal identity is puzzling to one whose thinking is not conditioned by exposure to the philosophical literature. How can personal identity be a problem? Isn't the identity of the person over time one of the most basic truths of all? Yes, it is basic, if by "basic" we understand that many other truths rest upon it as a presupposition, as any edifice rests upon its base. Recognizing this, one is forced to recognize that any significant modification to the concept of personal identity must be felt widely throughout the web of beliefs that depend upon it. It is foundational to our common-sense picture of ourselves in the world.

Looking at the matter more closely, we can see that the common-sense belief about personal identity—that it is just an obvious and "given" fact in need of no "theory" at all—carries within it a certain conception of what sort of thing persons are, what philosophers call an *ontology*. That is, when we talk of persons, we use the language of things, objects, individuals, *entities*. The most forthright expression of this ontology was Descartes' *res cogitans*, or "thinking thing." He identified this as the most certain truth at which the mind could rationally arrive: I am a thing which thinks.

Traditionally, there have been two theories that attempt to say what it is for a person to be the same person over time. They are the physical-continuity and mental-continuity theories. Both theories, as you can tell from their names, purport to explain the less understood sort of continuity, the continuity of persons, in terms of some presumably better understood continuity. Both therefore involve some assumptions about what a person is.

The physical-continuity theory says that a person is above all a physical organism in a functioning state. The identity of the person amounts to nothing more nor less than the identity of that physical organism. The mental-continuity theory claims that continuity of mental states is what counts. It is what is mental that is what is most directly connected to the identity of persons.

Both theories have a good share of intuitive appeal. The physical theorist argues that regardless of what philosophers might say in their more fanciful moments, no sane person would ever grant that some person claiming to be Uncle Charlie, despite being an obviously different physical individual, really *is* Uncle Charlie. If Uncle Charlie was a tall, heavyset black man when you last saw him, but the small Japanese woman at the door is claiming to be him, you will not say, "How do I know it's really you?" No, you will say that it is *impossible*, and you will shut the door. Nothing, insists the physical-continuity theorist, could possibly override this intuition, because physical organisms are just what persons are.

The mental-continuity theorist claims that the physical-continuity theorist is mistaking a practical conviction for theoretical insight. Consider, the mental-continuity theorist says, the fact that one can easily *imagine* (intelligibly) waking up one morning and looking in the bathroom mirror to discover that one has a new body. That we can imagine such a thing without running into any logical incoherence shows that at a deep level our concept of a person is not circumscribed by our concept of a person's physical body. If it were, the "new body" scenario would be literally unthinkable, which it clearly is not. It may be unthinkable in practice, in the light of current technologies, and this may count for the utility of the physical-continuity theory, but utility is not the same as truth.

Although physical continuity seems intuitively obvious, to say exactly what mental continuity amounts to is more of a chore. The "continuity of mental states" does not, in itself, say very much. John Locke offered that the relevant kind of mental continuity is provided by memory. It is memory that links the past experiences of an individual to her present consciousness in a way that they can be linked to no other (we may suppose for the moment) individual's present consciousness. Others have argued that in addition to memory there must be dispositional continuity. This means that a person is who he is not only in virtue of what he remembers, but also in virtue of how he characteristically responds to situations, people, ideas, and so forth.

As a way of pondering this, suppose that a "mindwipe" technology existed that had the effect of completely and permanently obliterating all of an individual's memories and personal dispositions, reducing him very nearly to a Lockean "blank slate," but without disrupting his organic health. Suppose further that in your society the mindwipe procedure is used as a "humane" alternative to capital punishment. You are given the choice: organic death by lethal injection or mindwipe. Which will it be?

It does not take long to realize that there is not much basis for choosing. One might prefer the mindwipe for reasons having to do with the well-being of other persons, such as loved ones,[1] but there doesn't seem to be much reason to prefer it for oneself. In what sense would one

---

1. Or organic death might be preferred for similar reasons.

be better off for being mindwiped? These morbid reflections support the notion that what matters in personal identity (and thus in survival) is some sort of mental continuity. If mental continuity is destroyed, physical continuity does not appear to be worth much.

There is substantial literature on the subject of mental continuity, illustrating the difficulty of making the very concept explicit. For our purposes, we need not rehearse these arguments. It will suffice to suppose that there is some workable account of mental continuity. If we later have reason to withdraw that supposition, so be it.

The physical-continuity theorist has not reached the end of possible arguments, however. He can offer a narrower version of the theory, according to which it is not the continuity of the entire body that matters but the continuity of the brain. He is driven to this position by a number of considerations. For one thing, it is clear that there are many modifications that one's body might undergo that would not underwrite a claim that an individual is "a different person." Amputations, cosmetic surgery, even sex-change surgery—all can involve drastic physical changes without tempting anyone to suppose that a loss of identity is involved. Furthermore, the "new body" scenario sketched above *is* convincing, and the physical-continuity theorist needs to say something about it.

What he can say is that most of the body—indeed, all of it except for the brain[2]—is peripheral, as far as personal identity is concerned. Thus, we can understand all manner of transformations of the body that don't affect personal identity, but we *can't* make sense of identity being preserved in a "new brain." A new brain would bring a new person into the picture.

The mental-continuity theorist is not finished either. She may ask the physical-continuity theorist, whom we may now call the brain-continuity theorist, why he is so concerned about the identity of the brain. He has by now taken a fairly breezy attitude about the other body parts, both individually and in sum. What is so special about the brain? The brain-continuity theorist cannot simply reply that the brain is the bit

---

2. And perhaps not even *all* of the brain. A case could be made that it is only the cerebral cortex that matters, but I shall not pursue that argument here.

that underlies personal identity; that would be a blatantly circular argument. What he must say instead is that the brain is the bit that underlies the very mental continuity that the mental-continuity theorist is so interested in. That is, brain continuity supports personal identity *because* it supports mental continuity. This is a proposition to which the mental-continuity theorist might well agree. It asserts that mental continuity is more basic to personal identity than physical continuity is, after all.

Things begin to get confusing here. It is tempting to suppose that the mental-continuity theorist is committed to some form of dualism, since she takes mental continuity to be something quite different from physical continuity. This temptation should be resisted, however. Although she may grant that mental continuity is quite different from physical continuity, that does not commit her to believing that there exists some nonphysical *entity* that has the mental continuity. Instead, she is claiming that mental continuity is not reducible to any particular physical continuity, whereas the brain-continuity theorist insists that it is.

It is at precisely this point in the dispute that it is interesting to consider the implications of artificial intelligence. In earlier chapters I have described and criticized a number of positions pertaining to the possibility of artificial mental states, but the Strong AI thesis remains the central claim. Recapitulating, the Strong AI thesis asserts that if a suitably programmed computer can pass the Turing Test, then we know all that we need to know to attribute the full range of mental states to it. A looser form of the thesis would state that regardless of what we may say about the Turing Test, a suitably programmed digital computer can instantiate mental states and, in fact, the mental states of persons are the result of the computational properties of the brain. The notion of "suitably programmed," on this looser view, need not be defined in terms of passing the Turing Test. This weaker thesis is sometimes referred to as "computationalism." Computationalism asserts no more than the Strong AI thesis does, but it does not commit itself to the logical adequacy of the Turing Test.

If computationalism is correct, a number of rather striking scenarios become plausible, at least in principle. Some of it may sound like science fiction, but the point is that computationalism, whatever its philosophical status, is already shaping much contemporary thinking about the mind, as in computational linguistics and computational psychology.

A computer executing a program is said to be doing a "process." As I have already described, the computer hardware is one physical object; the software is another physical object that interacts with the hardware in such a way as to modify its behavior, its process. If it is true that the mental states of a person are the result of computational properties of the brain, then a fair paraphrase would be that those mental states are the brain's process. A person, on this view, is an individual with a brain whose process includes various experiences causally structured over time in various ways by memory, intention, and disposition. For personal identity to obtain, this process must be continuous, allowing for certain temporary discontinuities such as sleep and unconsciousness. Again, let us suppose that we have a theory that describes the continuity and makes the allowances in a credible way. Personal identity is "process identity."

The trouble is that the identity of processes is by no means as clear and straightforward as the identity of discrete physical objects. For example, does process identity require physical continuity? Suppose I have a computer that plays chess. It is in the midst of a long search procedure, computing its next move. I employ a utility program to "freeze" the process while I do something else with the computer. When I put the computer back on the chess-move search, I think that no one would doubt that it is the "same process," resumed after a temporary suspension. This sort of suspension is an allowable discontinuity.

There are some programs that record and recall some of the things that happened to them the last time they were run. Their operation is cumulative. It makes some sense to say in such cases that it is the same process throughout. It makes sense in a way that it would not make sense if the program did *not* record and resume previous processes. In the latter case, where the process "starts from scratch" each time it runs, it makes more sense to say that there is one program but a series of processes. Now we can imagine that this cumulative program is stored on a floppy disk, where it also records its data each time it is run, so that it can pick up where it left off. It should make no difference to the identity of the process whether it is resumed on the same machine or a different machine, as long as it is a machine that can support the process (i.e., execute the software instructions). The point is that we can make sense of the notion of a single process spanning several "sessions" and physical realizations. If I am able to freeze my chess program in mid-search, record its state on a floppy disk, take the floppy disk home, and let my home computer pick up precisely where the program left off, there is no good reason to say that I have not "resumed" the process, as opposed to launching a new one.

If computationalism is true, it is in principle possible for me to transfer the functional state of my brain at some moment to another system of sufficient complexity to resume the process. As I lie on my deathbed, perhaps, I could request this procedure as my very last deed. In fact, all that would be required would be that a full record of my functional state be recorded in some storage medium; it could be transferred to a digital computer at some other time. When the transfer is accomplished and the process is "reactivated," the thesis at stake is that this new system *would be me*. No doubt the system would begin having experiences rather different from the ones that I had before (depending upon the nature of its input and output peripherals), but its mental states would be continuous with mine; they would pick up where mine left off, much as they do after a night's sleep. They would *be* my experiences.

It is certainly difficult to conceive of oneself, one's entire personality, memories, beliefs, and hopes as somehow "loaded" into the memory registers of a digital computer. Searle would respond that it is difficult because it makes no sense to begin with. The computationalist would ask if it is really so much easier to conceive of one's personality somehow "dwelling" in watery neural paste. He would add that we are imagining that it would somehow feel different to be "in" a computer, a concern that overlooks the premise that one's "program" has been completely transferred. Since how things feel is a function of that program, it follows that things will feel just the same as usual.

While the intuitions of some are such that they will never assent to the possibility of this scenario, it appears that there are many who find it plausible in principle. Perhaps it is because this sort of thing has been made passingly familiar through the imaginative efforts of science-fiction writers and filmmakers. Their imaginations, in turn, have been informed by their understanding of the achievements and conjectures of the computer scientists and others who ponder artificial intelligence. This is the cycle of conceptual fertilization that eventually transforms the landscape of thinking about the self. Computationalism offers nothing less than a kind of immortality. Once you are "defined" and captured in an algorithm and set of data records, your continued existence is no longer limited to the survival of a single physical system. As long as there are machines complex enough to receive you and execute your program, you will not perish.

This brave new worldview is not without its difficulties, however. For one thing, the computationalist conception of personal identity leads straight into the most vexing of all of the puzzles concerning identity: the problem of division.

Consider again the deathbed scenario mentioned above. Your organic human body is about to die, but you have arranged to have your entire mind offloaded to a high-capacity laser disk, later to be loaded into the computer brain of an android. You expect to continue "life" as that android. At the moment of physical death, the transfer takes place as planned. Next, however, there is an unexpected development. Instead of being loaded into a single android, a signal splitter is used and *two* androids are simultaneously programmed to resume *your* life. They are mechanically indistinguishable and now are also functionally indistinguishable. Perhaps you think: So much the better; now I'll have two bodies instead of one and will be able to experience twice as much.

But something is wrong. You had planned on only one android, and you had the conviction that that android would be *you*. Now there are two androids who cannot both be you. To suppose otherwise would be to violate one of the most basic canons of logical reasoning: the principle of transitivity of identity. If A and B are one and the same, and A and C are one and the same, then B and C must be one and the same. In this case, if A is you before your organic death, and B and C are the two androids who inherit your algorithmic soul, then B and C would have to be one and the same individual. But that makes no sense at all. B and C are two distinct individuals, no matter how much they resemble each other.

You had originally planned that just B would be around after your (that is, A's) bodily death. Computationalism convinced you that B would be not just an android remarkably like you, but rather would in every essential respect be you. The fact that C appears on the scene should not alter one whit whatever plausibility the notion that you would survive as B might have had. But C's appearance doesn't just alter that plausibility; it destroys it.

Something has gone wrong. According to computationalism, whatever justification there is for claiming that B is A is equally justification for claiming that C is A. But there can be *no* justification for the claim that B is C. We might simply conclude that this shows that computationalism is false. Logic forces this conclusion, in fact, unless perhaps computationalism can be modified in such a way that its consequences are less unpalatable.

Suppose we stipulate that you survive the process of offloading your mind if and only if your mind is offloaded to a single system. This way, we build into the concept of survival the requirement that there are no concurrent "implementations" of your program. On this view, uniqueness is essential to survival. This move certainly "solves" the problem of division—by forbidding it altogether. It's not a satisfactory solution, for a number of reasons. First, it is ad hoc. This can be explained by noting that uniqueness is not a property of a thing in itself but rather is a relational property, one that it has in virtue of being compared to other things. It seems odd to suppose that one's identity should depend not only upon one's own proper characteristics but also upon who else is or isn't around. This is directly connected to the second reason for thinking that the "uniqueness" requirement is not a satisfactory solution to the problem of division: After the completion of the mind-transfer process, you (or however we should designate the resultant being) would not even necessarily know if there were any rivals. In short, you would not know whether or not you had survived the process! If you were musing about

Descartes on your deathbed, and your last organic thought was, "I think . . . , " your next thought, in your transferred mind, might be, ". . . therefore I am, or maybe not."

I stated above that such consequences might be taken as sufficient to disqualify computationalism, unless they could be made unpalatable. We have seen that there does not seem to be any direct, nonarbitrary way to accomplish this. It is time to explore some *indirect* ways to make the consequences of computationalism less offensive.

One strategy is to point out that the division problem, as it has come to be called, is not the legacy of computationalism alone. The division problem infects any account of the person that explains mental continuity as the continuity of a *process* instead of an entity. It does not have to be a computational process. Processes have a fundamentally different ontology from entities; they are different sorts of beings altogether. In particular, a process can be divided without being halved. Processes are not subject to conservation principles in the same way that entities are.

A loaf of bread is an entity. If you and I are to share it we must divide it and, in so doing, halve it. A musical performance is an event. Suppose that this event takes place in a studio. It is broadcast over the radio so that you and I can "share" it by tuning in the broadcast on our stereo receivers. The event is "divided" in the sense that we are listening to the same music, but not in the sense that we ate the same loaf of bread. There is nothing puzzling here. It is more puzzling when we turn to the case of personal identity, because we are accustomed to thinking of ourselves as entities. The Christian conception of the soul, though not identical with that of the mind, is an entity-based conception. Plato seemed to favor a conception of the mind as an entity, although some of the pre-Socratic philosophers such as Heraclitus did not. We saw in Chapter 2 that the entity-based conception of mind crystallized in the work of Descartes and his notion of *res cogitans*. Though we may not be Cartesian dualists, this image has enough of a grip on us that we tend to insist upon a conception of personal identity that is violated by the division problem.

The other strategy is to argue that personal identity, rooted as it is in a conception of the person that cannot easily be defended, is not as important as we have thought. This is the position argued by the philosopher Derek Parfit. When we ponder the deathbed offloading procedure, we are concerned about whether we shall *survive* it. Because of the possibility of division, we cannot make clear sense of personal identity across such a transformation, so one response is to conclude that we do not survive. Parfit argues that a better response is to conclude that what the scenario shows is that what matters in questions of survival is not identity after all, but simply continuity. Since you cannot give a determinate answer to the question of whether the being that downloads your personality and memories will be you, the most perspicuous conclusion to draw is that what really matters in connection with survival is whether there is *anybody* who is your "continuant." That, says Parfit, is worthy of your concern in a way that the pure identity question is not.

Parfit is not arguing for or against computationalism or any other theory about artificial intelligence. The point here is that artificial intelligence, whatever one might think of its philosophical underpinnings, gives us a new and lucid way to conceive of an alternative to the conception of the person as an entity. Even if computationalism is wrong, it advances our ability to think about the person.

Persons as Machines

Once we construe the mind as a kind of computer or computer program, there are wider implications for our understanding of ourselves as persons, beyond the confines of particular traditional philosophical disputes. It is a commonplace observation that the image of the person that is reflected in culture is colored by the leading technologies of the day. To take the familiar example, Freud's psychodynamic model of the mind seemed to be shaped by metaphors of the steam engine: powerful "forces" of the Id "repressed" by the superego, and so forth. Even Descartes, for all his dualism, described the interaction between mind and body along the lines of a hydraulic system, a nexus of pumps and conduits through which "animal spirits" flowed.

These "models" of persons by persons may be seen as nothing more than metaphors, scaffolds from which we build and repair our inevitably incomplete understanding. Nevertheless, we must be cautious of speaking too lightly of "nothing more than" metaphors, as if these were mere ornaments of the understanding. At least some have argued that the metaphors we use tend to determine both what we regard as possible and what we take to be worthwhile. A few have warned that "artificial intelligence" as a metaphor for intelligence in general may be pointing us down a dark and narrow path indeed.

One of the first such voices of caution was that of Joseph Weizenbaum, the author of the program ELIZA, described in an earlier chapter. To remind you, this program was an early experiment in natural-language processing. By means of an ingenious set of rules, ELIZA simulated the utterances of a nondirective psychotherapist. What dismayed Weizenbaum, and eventually led him to write a book on the matter,[3] was the unexpected response to his experiment. He quotes, for example, an article in a medical journal:

> Further work must be done before the program will be ready for clinical use. If the method proves beneficial, then it would provide a therapeutic tool which can be made widely available to mental hospitals and psychiatric centers suffering a shortage of therapists. Because of the time-sharing capabilities of modern and future computers, several hundred patients an hour could be handled by a computer system designed for this purpose. The human therapist, involved in the design and operation of this system, would not be replaced, but would become a much more efficient man since his efforts would no longer be limited to the one-to-one patient-therapist ratio as now exists.[4]

The point of the quotation, of course, is that not only *could* psychotherapy be automated, but it *should* be. Weizenbaum eschews the question whether any such program will ever be technically "ready" (al-

---

3. Joseph Weizenbaum, *Computer Power and Human Reason* (San Francisco: W. H. Freeman, 1976).

4. K. M. Colby, J. B. Watt, and J. P. Gilbert, "A Computer Method of Psychotherapy: Preliminary Communication," *Journal of Nervous and Mental Disease*, 142, no. 2 (1966), pp. 148-52; quoted in Weizenbaum, *Computer Power*, p. 5.

though we have seen in earlier chapters that there are grounds for skepticism) and addresses instead the implications of the notion that this is a goal worth pursuing. Central to his position is the belief that the relationship between therapist and patient (or client, to use the currently preferred term) is just that: a relationship between human persons who share a set of concerns, hopes, and fears. To the extent that we are willing to substitute a programmed computer for the therapist, we are viewing the therapy problem as a technical problem, not a human one.

As we have seen, computers are automated formal systems. The problems that are most tractable by computers are problems that can be thoroughly formalized. In the idiom of an earlier chapter, the problem must define a specific task-world and set of algorithms for manipulating the objects in it. This was called a "formal theory." It is the willingness to see persons and the sorts of problems that bring them to psychotherapists in such terms that disturbs Weizenbaum.

A formal theory of the person and her problems is also implicitly a theory that the person and problems are formally definable. A theory, after all, is more than a neutral device for solving problems. It is a way of understanding, and it is part of the human commitment to theories that they tend to push into the margin anything that is not subsumed within them. They tend to ignore what they do not explain. As Weizenbaum wrote,

> The way theories make a difference in the world is thus not that they answer questions but that they guide and stimulate intelligent search. One use of a theory, then, is that it prepares the conceptual categories within which the theoretician and the practitioner will ask his questions and design his experiments.[5]

If the theory is about formalizing mental problems, then whatever resists formalization will be viewed as less and less significant. Weizenbaum uses the words "judgment" and "wisdom" to refer to the kinds of problem solving that we do in virtue of our being human persons

---

5.   Weizenbaum, *Computer Power*, p. 142.

who act in relationship to other human persons. Since the details of such relationships are far from understood, it is to be expected that they will resist formalization for a long time. That in itself is not a cause for concern. What *is* a cause for concern is the possibility that the commitment to the formalization and automation of psychotherapy will marginalize those relationships, both as objects of study and as ends in themselves.

Weizenbaum takes as an example the simple act of touching another person's hand. I say "simple" because in human terms it is indeed simple. To consider encoding the possible meanings of such a gesture in an algorithm and data structure is not so simple; it has components that are emotional, kinesthetic, and illocutionary, and it is utterly context-sensitive. Referring to such acts, Weizenbaum writes,

> Every symbolic representation of them must lose some information that is essential for some human purposes... [T]here are some things people come to know only as a consequence of having been treated as human beings by other human beings.[6]

Each time we as a culture decide to substitute computational power for human judgment, to attempt to automate it, we are pushing those things that Weizenbaum is referring to farther into the shadows. The price we pay for making our human problems tractable to computers is that we increasingly see ourselves as formal systems and become less capable of sustaining any other vision.

Hubert and Stuart Dreyfus, whose book *Mind over Machine* we have already encountered, come to similar conclusions about expert systems. Expert systems, you will recall, are computers programmed to solve problems in a narrow domain in a manner that is modeled upon the way human experts solve problems in that domain. They offer a five-stage model of the development of human expertise. The first stage is the "novice" stage, in which the novice learns to recognize certain objective features of the task domain in a context-free way. If the domain were medical diagnosis, for example, the novice stage is the

---

6. Ibid., p. 209.

stage at which the medical student learns to track simple measurements, such as blood pressure, pulse rate, and so on. At the second, or
"advanced beginner" stage, the novice's knowledge is supplemented by
experience. The aspiring diagnostician may come to recognize correlations between a patient's complexion, breathing pattern, or pupil dila-
tion and other more objective measurements. The third level is called
"competence"; it is the stage at which one begins to make judgments
about priorities. The medical student or practitioner begins to recognize
that certain signs and symptoms are more important to track than
others. The fourth stage is called "proficiency." Here, the practitioner
begins to develop an *intuitive* sense of priorities and procedures, while
still applying rule-following methods. She has a strong intuitive sense
of what to do, but continues to attempt to confirm her intuitions ana-
lytically. The fifth and final stage is "expertise."

> An expert generally knows what to do based on mature and practiced
> understanding. When deeply involved in coping with his environ-
> ment, he does not see problems in some detached way and work at
> solving them, nor does he worry about the future and devise plans.
> We usually don't make conscious deliberative decisions when we
> walk, talk, drive, or carry on most social activities. An expert's skill
> has become so much a part of him that he need be no more aware of
> it than he is aware of his own body.[7]

The farther one is from the novice stage, the less one relies upon
context-free features of the situation for making decisions and the more
one relies upon "judgment." As we have already seen, the symbolic-processing approach to AI—the approach taken in expert systems—involves
manipulating tokens that correspond to context-free objects in the task-
world. These objects are context-free because that is precisely what the
formal description of a task-world is all about.

To the extent that a task requires interpretation of contexts, it
requires judgment and will therefore be resistant to the expert system's
modeling approach, or "knowledge engineering," as it is sometimes

---

7.   Dreyfus and Dreyfus, *Mind over Machine*, p. 30.

called. The word "resistant" is vague. The point of these remarks is not that certain areas of human expertise must lie forever beyond the reach of automated expert systems. That may be so, but it would be very difficult to prove. Furthermore, as things stand, there are already expert systems that do useful work at at least the level of what Dreyfus and Dreyfus call competence; there is every reason to believe that such systems will be improved.

These achievements carry certain costs. As is always the case with costs, we are better off if we can identify them. One cost is the possibility that as we come to trust expert systems we shall become less interested in and ultimately less trusting of human expertise. If that happens, there is a real danger that the program-resistant part of the domain—the part that has been transmitted by apprenticeship—will be lost. Typesetting is an example of a craft that has been rendered largely obsolete by the almost universal use of automated expert systems. That is the smaller part of the cost, however, and it is one that is attached to every technological advance. Skills that were once important, whose adepts may have reached high levels of mastery, suddenly become defunct and are preserved, if at all, only in the most antiquarian sense of "preservation." At the same time, new crafts emerge, with new possibilities to be explored.

The real cost is the one we pay if we become so bewitched by the success (in both performance and financial terms) of expert systems that we begin to see every form of human expertise as essentially computational. In that light, we might well come to distrust what is not computational and to collapse our sense of rationality itself to obedience to an algorithm.

Moving away from expert systems, we turn to some observations by Sherry Turkle in her influential book *The Second Self*.[8] In the first chapter, Turkle discusses her experience interviewing "child philosophers," children whose concepts of living things and persons have been formed during a childhood that includes fairly extensive interaction with

---

8. Sherry Turkle, *The Second Self: Computers and the Human Spirit* (New York: Simon & Schuster, 1984).

computers, as well as media images of them. At a very early age, as they are outwitted by computer-driven games, children come to recognize them as "smart" and tend to think of them as alive in some sense. In later childhood, however, they establish a sense of their own personal distinctness from computers. Although they readily grant intelligence to these machines, they tend to insist that they lack emotions and thus are not quite authentic living beings. Turkle concludes with a good-news/bad-news set of comments:

> There is an element in all of this that many will find surprising and reassuring. Children's adaptation to the computer contrasts with a prevalent fear that involvement with computers inevitably leads to a more mechanical way of thinking about psychology, perhaps even to a mechanized view of people. Faced with a machine, children, at least, seem to resist seeing people as like it: they see people as essentially what it is not.[9]

That is the good news. Children have not, so far, tended to *identify* themselves as machines, or to identify machines as persons. The bad news comes just a few paragraphs later, as Turkle comments on the similarity of the children's way of thinking with the nineteenth-century Romantics' belief in the dichotomy of humankind's rational and passional natures.

> Children growing up in a computational culture face a similar danger. Their easy acceptance of the idea that computers closely resemble people in their "thinking" and differ only in their lack of "feeling" supports a dichotomized view of human psychology.
> Thought and feeling are inseparable. When they are torn from their complex relationship with each other and improperly defined as mutually exclusive, the cognitive can become mere logical process, the cold, dry, and lifeless, and the affective is reduced to the visceral, the primitive, and the unanalyzable.[10]

The "dichotomized" conception of the person trivializes the intellect

9.   Ibid., p. 62.
10. Ibid., p. 63.

and the emotions. It relinquishes any notion of rationality that is more than the capacity of following algorithms and leaves little role for the emotions beyond a kind of animal accompaniment to such processing.

Our response should not be to wring our hands but to try to understand. Something called "computer literacy" is widely acknowledged as an important set of skills in what is coming to be called an "information age." But even as we are awash in these metaphors, we must recognize that the real challenge is understanding. Computer literacy means much more than knowing how to use a spreadsheet or write a macro. It means encountering the *meaning* of computing technology as it crystallizes in literature, philosophy, and popular culture. Artificial intelligence is the central metaphor that this literacy must interpret and deconstruct. That is, we need to come to understand the conditions of the very intelligibility of artifical intelligence, the conditions under which it is possible for computational metaphors to take root. Artificial intelligence has surfaced before in the history of ideas, from the mythical golem of Jewish folklore to the pathetic—and far from emotionless—creation of Mary Shelley's Doctor Frankenstein. But the mind in the machine may turn out to be the symbolic image that is most emblematic of our own century, perhaps more so than the mushroom cloud.

Index

U

Unger, Peter, 120

V

Verification principle, 38–39
Vienna circle, 37
von Neumann, John, 7

W

Weak AI thesis, 15, 79
Weizenbaum, Joseph, 10, 87, 163–65
Whitehead, 1
Winograd, Terry, 11